EERIE TALES
OF
SOUTH WALES

By
Hayley Williams

ISBN: 978-1-8380752-5-5

First published in print form in the United Kingdom in 2020 by
Cambria Publishing.

See our other titles on our website at: cambriabooks.co.uk

Dedicated to my beloved husband
Andrew who passed away 18th May 2018

CONTENTS

Introduction

I have been fascinated with all things paranormal for the majority of my life, as my mother would often state that she could see dead relatives in baffling ways. My interest probably stems back to tales of my maternal ancestors who were well known throughout Pencoed, Llanharan and Brynna in South Wales for their spooky experiences and predictions. In fact, the first know person gifted with this unusual talent was my distant Auntie Megan, who was a white witch who made herbal remedies to cure sick animals. This type of witch is in no way connected to the darker side of making spells: as this disturbing form of worship is where the departed from the lower realms of the spirit world are encouraged to make contact with the human race. This could also result in the performing of human sacrifice through the act of a séance. This requires a group of people seated around a table (usually round), joining hands and the closing of the eyes in the hope of contacting the dead. One person will then ask questions towards the outer world, waiting for a response in the form of knocks, sounds or bangs. Sometimes a downturned glass will be placed in the centre of the table with all from the group placing their index finger gently upon it before questions are asked. If a spirit is present, the glass should move freely on its own accord, draining the energy from the living through the vibrations of the finger.

Objects have been known to be thrown or moved by unseen hands in some instances. This type of movement is known as poltergeist activity and the lingering spirit can often take over the bodily actions of the living. This, in my opinion, spells out danger and something which I would not recommend. Another dangerous means of contacting the dead is by placing letters of the alphabet and numbers around the rim of the table and asking the ghost to spell out their name by the movement of the glass. This type of communication is known as the Ouija and is extremely perilous and must not be performed as a means of entertainment.

Further down the line of my descendants, my great grandmother, Elizabeth Hancock, used to predict the future by eerily glaring into the flames of the open fire in the hearth, thus foretelling people's destiny. She was a popular figure throughout the community of Llanharan where neighbours would eagerly await her predictions through the reading of their tea leaves in the bottom of their teacup. She is believed to have been an accurate reader with her mystic powers.

My great grandfather, William Stallard, was a psychic medium who regularly attended spiritualist meetings in Brynna.

My more intense interest in the spirit world occurred in 2004, after the devastating experience of losing both of my grandmothers within 2 weeks of each other. I came into contact with someone from a paranormal forum and he persuaded me to write for his website on the history and ghostly happenings on the Isle of Wight, an island part of the British Isles many miles from my own abode. It was fascinating to discover information about a place which I had no official connection and I became embroiled with my task, which helped me to overcome my grief. Writing in such in-depth ways on an area which I had never visited, gave me the incentive to explore the history and ghostly tales of Porthcawl, the place where I live.

In March 2006, the Porthcawl Paranormal Team formed and it was our intention to seek out the ghosts who loiter around this modern seaside town. Ghosts and the paranormal go hand in hand and had become popular again through the power of television and we believed that local coverage on the subject was needed. The newly formed team all set off on our first mission equip with a thermometer, temperature gauge, compass, EMF reader, stills and video cameras. An eerie lane in Nottage was our first location and since then we discovered the ghostly happenings around public houses and other places of interest throughout Porthcawl and other towns and villages beyond.

This book is a collaboration of my Spooky Tales column for The Glamorgan Gem which was a free local newspaper. It includes many interesting towns and villages from around the counties of Bridgend, The Vale of Glamorgan, Rhondda Cynon Taf and Newport, with an interesting selection of history, legends and ghostly tales.

A view of Porthcawl from Stormy Down with Ogmore By Sea to the left

County of Bridgend

Bridgend Town

The old market town of Bridgend (Ogwr, or Pen-y-bont in Welsh meaning head of the bridge on the Ogmore) lies 25 miles west of Cardiff and dates back to 16th Century. Features of this once bustling town include tanneries, a wool mill (where its manager lived in a house in Brewery Lane in 1790s close to the site of the modern-day rugby club) and potteries. The Ogmore River flows freely through the town and was once used by pilgrims who waded through its waters towards their destination of Pembrokeshire.

It is believed that Bridgend acquired its name from the majestic old bridge which was originally built in 1425 where a pilgrim ford was a formidable attribute. The bridge linked the north and south banks, giving locals easy access to destinations otherwise alien in terms of reaching ability.

The bridge was constructed with 4 arches which was partially destroyed by flooding in 1775, with half of its arches gobbled up by the swollen river. It was eventually rebuilt. Its most recent restoration took place in 2005/06.

In 18th Century, a Victorian market hall was built around the area of the modern Rhiw Shopping Centre. Sadly it is now a distant memory but the market bell is still visible at its entrance.

Bridgend contained a few quarries too, together with an engine works and large farmers market at its centre. The market ceased trading in 1970s.

During WWII Bridgend played its own part in the

dangers of war. On its outskirts, a prisoner of war camp named Island Farm housed American Soldiers for a short time before being used for German prisoners of war. It served as a secure unit over a 4 year period with almost 2000 high-ranking German soldiers inhabiting the shelters, its most famous inmate being Field Marshal Gerd Von Rundstedt. However, Island Farm is most widely remembered for 67 prisoners escaping by tunnelling their getaway on 10th March 1945. They were all captured within 8 days of their escape.

Bridgend town itself did not evade natural tragedies, as the River Ogmore burst its banks and flooded the town in 1960. This was when the Welsh Water Authority built flood defence walls of concrete to prevent further catastrophes happening again.

Bridgend Town is not without its Grade II listed buildings either. Listed means that premises are protected from demolition or alteration. There are plenty of old buildings throughout the borough and these include Coed Parc (once the Headquarters of Mid Glamorgan County Libraries), Herman Chapel on Nolton Street, the milepost in Caroline Street, the buildings once used as Preswylfa Children's Homes in Merthyr Mawr Road, Randall Memorial Drinking Fountain in Wotton Street, the old Police Station, the old Workhouse (Bridgend General Hospital) and the War Memorial to name but a few.

Tales of folklore are quite abundant throughout Wales and Bridgend is no exception as it still seems to be a gathering place of legends from a bygone era.

The eerie sight of two men speaking in foreign tongue has been witnessed loitering around the old prisoner of war camp. Their ghostly figures then mysteriously fade into oblivion as if reluctant to be recognised. Could these strange gentlemen be unwilling to forget the perils of capture, unable to take their rightful place beyond our realm?

Seemingly unaware of witnesses, a lifelike washer woman wearing green clothing with prominent webbed feet has been seen beneath the second arch of the old bridge. She seems to obliviously carry on with her chores before vanishing into thin air. But who could this strange lady be and why does she seem intent on completing tasks from an age beyond our understanding and confusing the living?

The unusual sighting of a small grey horse with unrecognizable people sitting upon its back has been seen. Said to gallop through the water and then fly off into the skies, it has been known to terrify spectators. This type of creature is known as the Waterhorse. But could it be from a tale of Celtic folklore where the Ceffyl-dawr preys upon the innocent, hoping to torment their minds into confusion. Or maybe it is a long gone fairytale image lost in the depths of time.

Coity Castle

First thought to be erected using wood after the Norman Conquest of 1066, the Lordship of Coity, Payn de Turbeville gained control of Coity castle during the 12th Century. Nicknamed 'The Demon' he was responsible for the circular embankment, deep ditch and gatehouse, making it a timber fortification. During 1180s Sir Gilbert de Turbeville rebuilt the castle using stone and included a keep, curtain wall, Inner Bailey and northeast tower which spanned 3 stories.

It was during the 14th Century that the castle altered once more, giving it more of a grandeur appearance. A striking annex to the northeast became equip with windows, a fireplace and latrines/toilet areas. A central pier was also added to support the upper floors.

Other important names connected with the castle

include Sir Lawrence Berkerolles (1384) who married into the descending de Turbeville family line. The Gamage family inherited the castle after the death of Sir Lawrence Berkerolles in 1411 and Sir Robert Sydney, Earl of Leicester, whose descendants continued to own the castle until the 19th Century took over the castle. There are few battles known to have taken place at the castle, but encounters between the Normans and the Welsh and Owain Glyndwr, who was a freedom fighter for the Welsh during the 15th Century are well documented. Although he attacked Coity castle, he failed to take control.

Legend maintains that Payn de Turbeville was a philanderer who enjoyed visiting his lovers during the hours of darkness, leaving his own guards on patrol. On one particular evening, his wife Sybil disposed of her husband's guards, consigning her own defence force instead. On Payn de Turbeville's return they refused to give him access to the castle, therefore leaving him outside, alone and in the pouring rain. What happened to him after that is a mystery, but could he have perished outside his own abode?

The chilling vision of a disembodied soldier has been sighted appearing to have no eyes. Could this gallantry man be a victim of battles from a distant era?

Hooded shadows have been witnessed stalking the grounds of the castle as if lost in time. Why would monk-like figures want to associate themselves with a building which would have no relevance to their own existence?

The silhouette of a lady has been seen at the dead of night gazing from the window of the tower as if trapped. Who could this lady be and is she waiting for a knight in shining armour to rescue her from a fate beyond her power?

Eerie light anomalies (orbs) have often been seen by bystanders floating around the gatehouse before disappearing into oblivion. Could these unusual lights be the spiritual energy of a past occupier unable to communicate with the living, or an illusion of imagination?

Dunraven Gardens

Situated on a hill overlooking the beach of Southerndown, lies the walled gardens of Dunraven. The history surrounding these gardens has an intriguing insight into a world of Lordship and tragedy, connected to a building of grandeur from our not too distant past.

The fortified manor house known as Dunraven Castle once stood overlooking the coast of Southerndown. It was built on the site of an Iron Age settlement and fort on the hillside, which later made way for a 12th Century stone building constructed by Armand Botteler (also interpreted as Botiler). During 16th Century, the Vaughan family lived within the manor house until 1642 when the Wyndham kinfolk purchased the property. They became important citizens within the community and built a fortified manor, naming it Dunraven Castle. Its ancient name in Welsh is Dundryfan, which translates as triangular fortress.

Ancient Princes of Soluria, Bran ap Llyr, his son Caradoc and other families from Ireland also lived at the fortified manor and 1886 the Duke and Duchess of Tick visited the dancing stones of Dunraven.

During World War I, the manor was used as a military hospital and convalescent home for wounded soldiers from the ill-fated battle. Before the outbreak of World War II, the castle played host to the Dunraven Horticultural and Flower Show, where educational walks were organized around its beautiful grounds and gardens. The castle then continued as a family home until the 1960s, when the owner had a dispute with the local authority because they refused him permission to develop the land. In a fit of anger, he demolished the building in 1962. But tragedy had already cast its spell on him as his 3 sons had met their deaths in tragic circumstances.

Today, only the enclosed walled gardens, entrance gateway, grand lodge, outer wall, ice tower and ruins remain of this once enchanting fortified manor. These are all now treasured as Grade II listed.

Legend maintains that Walter Vaughan, who was Lord of Dunraven, was a kind-hearted man who found satisfaction in saving the lives of sailors whose vessels had become victim to the dangerous sea. His heroics were frowned upon by the government, causing him to become disillusioned and as a result he spent his fortune in a wasteful way. Penniless, he teamed up with the local wreckers and their pirate leader named Mat of the Iron Hand and together they lured ships onto the treacherous rocks by evilly placing lanterns on roaming sheep. They were used as decoys to confuse sailors whose vessels would plunge onto the hazardous rocks.

Walter Vaughan had been a magistrate in previous years and it was him who passed sentence upon Mat of the Iron Hand and now he was indulging in the same circle of wickedness as the pirate and his ship wreckers. Burdened by his greed for fortune and time spent away from his home, Walter tragically lost his 3 sons who all drowned at sea. Could these horrifying accidents be the result of fate paying him back with heartache for his dastardly deeds, or just a legendary fable passed on through time?

The glowing figure of a ghostly lady wearing a blue dress and leaving behind the distinct aroma of perfume was reported to haunt the upper floors of the fortified manor for centuries before its downfall. It is not known who she was, but could she have been responsible for the misfortune surrounding the manor, by showing her cursed disapproval in such a disturbing way?

Invisible but chilling screams have been heard, bellowing out across Dunraven Bay, pitifully shouting for help, which could only have fallen upon deaf years from a bygone era, when looters gleefully watched the harrowing ordeal of sailors drowning in the cruel sea. Could these haunting sounds be from a restless seaman who walks the coastline on the anniversary of his death, or just a mass figment of imagination?

Around the 'Ice Tower' the echoing sound of horses galloping at pace has been heard, particularly at the dead of night when no physical creatures would be free to roam. Could this distinct noise be an eerie reminder of the labours of our past, unwilling to make way for the present?

Kenfig and Maudlam

The ancient Borough of Kenfig dates back to around 2000 BC. It was linked to the Romans and was a thriving town encased within high walls to protect it from enemy attack. It is steeped in history and legends which are fascinating tales about the town's actual existence. Kenfig castle and original town were buried under the sand mountains during the medieval period after a raging storm towards another old town called Margam, which is situated near Port Talbot. Other theories suggest that Kenfig dates back to 2000 BC as reminders of the Bronze Age have been identified. These include a burial site within the surrounding area. Although many believe that they lie beneath Kenfig pool/lake, which gobbled up its town and people.

It was during Elizabethan times that some documentation alleged that the old town was situated near the ruins of the old castle, whereas another revelation stated that the city sank beneath the pool itself, which is another confusing story to the people of today.

Evidence of Kenfig's history is still displayed through its buildings, which include the Church of Mary Magdelaine in Maudlam, the Angel Inn, Maudlam, The

Prince of Wales public house and its scattered cottages and farms.

Legend maintains that Kenfig pool is bottomless, as this was the belief after a man, his horse and carriage became entangled in the ruins of the old town beneath the menacing waters when riding through it. The fable insists they were never seen again.

Myth states that a fierce whirlpool sucks people into its funnel of swirling water, swallowing them up as if satisfying its hunger. Could this unlikely fable be an invention from the pool's humble beginnings, or an 'old wives tale' told to families from a bygone era gathered around the fireplace listening to stories from their elders?

Eerie screams have been heard at the dead of night bellowing out across the wilderness. Could these frightful sounds be from a young man from the Victorian era who drowned in Kenfig river after falling from a tree, or the gwrach y rhibyn (hag of the mist) echoing her spell of wickedness.

Sightings of a white horse on moonlit nights have been identified cantering across the wilderness only to vanish into thin air. Could this phantom appearance be a remembrance of the romantic tragedy linked to the Maid of Sker?

On the distant seas towards Sker rocks, a ghostly ship has been seen mirroring white mist around it, particularly on stormy nights, when the Church bells beneath the pool will distinctly ring out. Could these scary happenings be a reenactment of a ship lost to the treacherous seas when the bells would ring out warning its people of disaster?

The figure of a phantom lady wearing an old fashioned flowing gown has been seen dancing across the land before disappearing into the darkness. Could this seemingly happy lady be connected to the annual dancing festivals which were held at the local guildhall, or just an illusion lost in the midst of time?

Kenfig Hill

The community of Kenfig Hill lies 1 mile north east of Pyle and 6 miles from Bridgend. It is not listed to be of great age, but does have documentation regarding an Iron Age hill fort on its surrounding hills. In later times the area was known for its mushroom growth as it was probably barren land.

Kenfig Hill grew as a town when a coal mine opened giving employment to locals. Also the Pyle and Kenfig railway gave its people freedom to travel as the line passed under Pisgah and Bridge Streets. In more traditional times, the Gaiety cinema was opened in the Miners Welfare Hall in Pyle, as well as many individual shops and amenities. The town was also known for its annual carnival, where excited residents would dress up to parade the streets.

Unfortunately in 1892, an accident at the coal slip devastated the community as 112 men and boys perished in the horrifying tragedy. Locals to this day pay tribute to the victims.

There seems to be very few of tales of the supernatural around Kenfig Hill, but one account involves a young boy of around 7 or 8 years of age, who tragically died of disease. He loved music and enjoyed playing the piano during his time on earth. In the Victorian era, playing instruments and finding other modes of entertainment were popular, as there was no electricity or comforts as we enjoy today. The unusual sound of a piano playing hymns has been heard in the corner of the living room of a dwelling within the area during the evenings, even though there is nothing of this nature within the household. Loud footsteps on the upper floors would also become apparent, sending modern residents into a frenzy of fear, especially as no physical person would be on the upper floors at the time. Could this innocent boy be reminding the living of his time of earth, vying to be remembered with his old fashioned entertainment?

Cefn Cribbwr

The Hamlet of Cefn Cribbwr is 5 miles northwest of Bridgend and lies on a ridge. It was originally thought to have been part of Higher Tythegson, as roaming grassland connected the two together during times gone by. Earthworks of an ancient settlement can be seen to the West of the vicinity. The ridge also proudly administered the Bedford Ironworks during the Industrial Revolution.

Legend maintains that a dastardly gang of men who called themselves the 'Cefn Riders and Red Goblins' were rampant throughout the district and renowned in local folklore. They may have been linked to the ancient Britons who built a camp or fort called Castell Kribor as a defence against intruders. They were ruthless individuals, but by the 19th Century people who lived in the lowlands began to trust them. However, due to conditions changing along the land on the ridge with the soil becoming poor, the gang descended to the lowlands and became menacing towards the locals, attacking them, taking what they required and sending fear amongst the innocent. Farms would be ransacked and livestock would disappear. They also attacked strangers and packmen to steal their wares in a thuggish way.

The Cefn Riders would spread fear mostly on foot, but would often show no mercy on anyone, and one particular victim was leapt upon and forced to carry one of the Riders on his back to loot unsuspecting victims. What became of these ruthless people remains a mystery, but it is hoped that they were punished for their endeavours.

Another mythical tale involves Cribwr the Giant. He is thought to have lived in Castell Cefn Cribbwr in Morgannwg. A mystery man called Arthur killed his three sisters and then slayed the Giantess. Arthur nicknamed himself 'Hot Pottage' as he found the killings amusing: Hot Pottage for the first killing, Warm Porridge for the second and Morsel of bread was the third. The Giantess escaped the dubbed name.

When Cribwr reprimanded Arthur for his actions, he replied: ***Cribwr take the combs And cease with currish anger If I get a real chance - surely What they have had, thou shalt have to.***

Could this account of a giant (who may have been just an extremely tall man) be a legend passed down through the generations, or is it a real story grossly emphasised for pleasure?

Cefn Cribwr Signal Junction

This disused signal box, or junction as it is also known, was built in 1898. It stands in a lonely location down an eerie lane with only the wildlife to keep it company.

In 1825, prior to the steam railway being built, a horse-drawn tramroad was constructed to carry coal and iron from Maesteg to the new Porthcawl Dockyard.

A gentleman called Walter Curl was working on the lever in the downstairs area of the building one night, when he slipped off a ladder knocking his head on the fireguard a few feet below, tragically breaking his neck. His ghost is reported to haunt the signal junction during the middle of the night, when the wind will mysteriously howl and the windows rattle as if the spirit of this man is trying to get in. If these eerie actions are from Walter Curl, why would he want to return to a place where he met his end?

On a cold and dark evening in February, Tracey Walmsley and I were invited to investigate the signal junction. The darkness engulfed us with anticipation as the visual memorabilia outside as well as in was a reminder of the buildings active past. The spooky lane leading to our destination was littered with the odd railway truck in the verges of its secluded surroundings and rail sleepers could also be vividly seen hiding as if redundant. The signal junction itself seemed isolated in the darkness and we were eager to start the investigation. We were eternally grateful to Keith Morgan who drove us to this location and to John Mason and his wife Carol who made us feel welcome.

Our baseline test revealed some unexplained hotspots, which particularly occurred around the now abandoned levers. The presence of a lady was briefly felt around the milk churn within that area, but she seemed to have connections with a now demolished property. Could this lady be the wife of a signalman from its days of another era?

The sensation of an angry man was also felt. He seemed to be in a rage with someone from his time and the name Charles became relevant all of a sudden. Could this angry man be connected to a heated exchange between two men from two different signal junctions from yesteryear, or just another restless soul unhappy with our presence?

Our equipment batteries seemed to drain periodically for no apparent reason, only to recharge in an instant. Could the ghostly beings that seemingly haunt the signal junction be trying to tell us to leave their former workplace, unhappy that we were encroaching on their territory?

Our investigation was an adventure of nostalgia and although we did not find any concrete evidence of spiritual activity, we felt satisfied that our visit was memorable for such an interesting location.

Laleston

The village of Laleston is situated 2 miles west of Bridgend and on the edge of the Vale, with landmarks which enhance its character. Its origins date back to Norman landowners named Lageles, Lachelston or Laheles and the terrain was then presented to the Monks of Margam Abbey by the family. The village probably has its origins back to earlier times as nearby fields leading to Tythegston, to the South West, boast a chambered tomb from the Neolithic period named Cae Tor which is a buried Mesolithic monument from 2500 – 2000 BC. Unfortunately, the tomb was never properly investigated for archaeological purposes.

Laleston Milestone

An ancient landmark is the milepost on the High Street, which was listed in 1998 as Grade II. It was erected during 1830s for the Bridgend Turnpike Trust in elaborate detail showing directions to various towns and cities such as

London, which had a proposed distance on 179 miles. The road itself and its turnpike (toll road) were positioned in 1764.

The former Horeb Presbyterian Church is a 19th Century building and Grade II listed from 1990, is now used as an independent school.

Legendary tales are common in villages and Laleston is no exception. One of interest involves a man who collapsed outside one of the 3 public houses which donned the High Street. The landlord of the first quickly gave the man a stiff brandy which promptly revived him and then he continued on his way. Sadly the same occurrence happened outside the second public house called The Bell (once situated in front of the Church) and the landlord here gave him another brandy. However, the landlord of the third pub (Oystercatcher) emptied a bucket of water over him. The man was last seen running towards Bridgend, never to be seen in the flesh again. But, the lifelike ghostly image of a man dressed in old-fashioned clothing has been spotted wandering up the street only to disappear in a hazy mist. Could this be the gentleman returning for his dose of brandy?

Another Welsh tale of folklore involves the Saracen mason and architect Lalys, who after being captured from the Crusades, was compelled to build a church at nearby Llangewdd. Irate at being forced to perform such a task, his legacy lives on in the form of disembodied hands leafing through a non-existent book around the area of his long forgotten Church.

Around the Church, at the dead of night, the phantom sound of congregational singing has eerily been heard. Could the people of yesteryear be chanting their hymns in the hope of being heard by the innocents of today?

In the fields beyond the Laleston Inn, the strange vision of an unusual white animal has been seen. Described as

17

resembling a cross between a deer and a big cat, could this peculiar creature be lost in the midst of time, or just an illusion?

The spine-chilling echo of a stagecoach travelling at pace has been heard, tearing down an imaginary lane at dusk, forcing bystanders to violently jump from its path, only to discover that nothing of this nature is travelling through. Could this frightful noise be a hurried re-enactment from a bygone era when horse and carriage was the only means of transport?

Legend maintains that the burial tombs of Tythegston are cloaked with secrecy, magic and myth and an intriguing tale involves the shoeing of horses around the area of the mound. These good-natured animals would be left alone for a short period of time, in order for their master to prepare for the task of giving them new shoes. On his return, the horse is said to have been mysteriously shod and the silver coins of payment gone. Was this tale of folklore linked to fairy magic?

There are many legends, or even myths, rebounding from such chambers of an ancient era, which include spending time after nightfall at the sinister tomb. Performing such a vigil would result in that person either going raving mad, becoming a victim of instant death, or emerging as a poet. The mound or mountain top and its surrounding stones were believed to be women who had been cast into stone for dancing on the Sabbath day, a macabre belief shrouded in mystery. Could this legend be the reason for a person's downfall?

Burial chambers have also been known to have adopted the name snivelling corner as the tears of the mourners are said to echo through the chamber and its stones are believed to be weeping. But could these tales be true, or merely a mass illusion from ancient times?

Laleston was the centre of Christian worship from around 1173, with records relating to Tewkesbury Abbey. A raised pre-Norman circular Churchyard and Church built possibly of mud with two mysterious headstones from 11 – 12 Century were located within the vicinity. The Church was dedicated to St. Cewydd and in 1180, William, Earl of Gloucester, granted the land to William Lageles of Laleston.

The modern Church of St. David was listed as a Grade I monument in 1963 and dominates the village. It was constructed around 13 – 14 Centuries. It contained a nave, chancel, a proportional tower and south porch. It was restored in 1871 by John Pritchard, who probably laid the floor 18 inches higher that its original base as burials were permitted inside the Church between 1650 and 1750. It also incorporated Cliff Cottage in 18th Century.

The Church of the present day, at the heart of the village, stands inside its almost circular Churchyard which is enclosed within rubble walls with a wrought iron gate. The Churchyard contains a Grade II listed medieval period Cross, which could have been the focus of a preaching site.

Tythegston

The small community of Tythegston is in the Cwmwd of Tir yr Hwndrwd, Cantref of Cron Neddm, or the Hundred of Newcastle. It is on the outskirts of Porthcawl on the road to Laleston and is around 4 miles from the town of Bridgend as its visible milestone declares. This 1640 Parish monument also states that it is 181 miles from the city of London, the capital city of Great Britain.

Tythegston lies off the main road to Porthcawl and comprises of a few quaint cottages, dwellings and farms, just a small distance from the distinguished Tythegston Court.

Tythegston Court was the medieval strong house of the

Turbeville family of Coity in the early 14th Century. But this 16th Century mansion, once described as Tower House, is Grade II listed and took its present form in 1769 when the medieval building and its rectangular tower were retained and heightened. Some of its original features still exist such as the drip-stones over the kitchen window at the back of the house which face the 18 Century Courtyard and a few doors from a 'shadow library'.

The 15th Century Ty Mansion Tower was the home of Margarit, Lady Malefaunt, who was allegedly abducted, imprisoned there and starved for 2 days. This was because Lewse Leyshon handed her a counterfeit letter stating that enemies lay in wait for her and her life was at risk. His untrue statement and dubious plan was to force her hand in marriage to him after the death of her husband. Instead (not wanting to do so) Lady Malefaunt fled to London to live with her mother 'by wise governance'.

Another story relating to Tythegston reveals events leading up to a violent clash between two land owners Henry Knight of Tythegston and Thomas Bennet of Laleston. It was settled by the Great Sessions of Glamorgan in April 1770 as duels of this nature were forbidden in this country at the time, as they were deemed to be within breach of the peace. The quarrel was over money and land; the result of which saw Knight pay Bennet 1 Shilling and ten pence per year to rent Tythegston Court.

By marriage, Tythegston Court was then passed to the Lougher family of Sker, who also has residence at Ty Mawr, (now Nottage Court) in the 16th Century. This is because the Lougher heiress married Edward Turbeville of Sutton and has since come down the generations to the present day.

The small Church of St. Tyddwg can be seen from the road within its locality and was built on the site of an ancient Church which was originally a Chapel belonging to

Newcastle in Bridgend from 13th Century. The new Church was built in Perpendicular style with a chancel, nave, south porch and western bell turret. This quaint little Church with its dainty spire can be seen across the landscape.

Between Laleston and Tythegston across a few fields and over stiles near the main road into Porthcawl and towards woodland, the spectacular sight of a Neolithic long barrow or Chambered Cairn can be seen. It is situated towards the East end of a long mound.

Traditionally a Chambered Cairn is a burial monument, usually constructed during the Neolithic/Megolithic period. It is often built using a mound of stones inside which is a sizeable chamber for the burial of their loved ones. Some chambered cairns are also passage-graves and can be described as barrows. The best view of it is from the site of Tythegston Church, although reaching them may be a little harder.

Llangynwd

The old parish of Llangynwd lies on the top of a ridge overlooking the Llynfi Valley. Thought to house the oldest Inn in South Wales, the Yr Hen Dy was built during ancient times.

Llangynwd is another example of being in the hands of the Norman Lords of Glamorgan from the 12th Century. Documents from the 13th Century state that a castle named 'Castell Coch' was built around 1246, neglected by Llewelyn ap Iorwerth and later described as *a castle burnt in the war*. This fortress was built on the site of an older building where earthworks are still visible around the landscape. Evidence of Roman occupation has also been unearthed, with ditches, ramparts and traces of camps.

The mother Church of Maesteg is dedicated to St. Cynwyd, son of Cynfel with connections in the midst of

Llancarfan, as a gift from somebody with the initials E. P. of Tondu (possibly Powell) from 1686. Although St. Cynwyd is said to have founded Llangynwd, there is evidence of the village dating back to 2000 BC. Iron Age earthworks can be seen outlined on the hillside, together with the Bodvac Stone displaying writings in Latin 'Bodvocus – he lies here, the son of Catotigirus, great-grandson Eternalis Vedomas'. This inscription probably dates from 550 AD.

Llangynwd Church accommodates a Celtic Cross and in the Chancel, a brass plate is the dedicated resting place of the legendary Ann Thomas, Maid of Cefn Ydfa. The Church itself was restored in 1893.

During the middle ages and up to the 17th Century, Llangynwd has associations with the Chief Bards of Tir Brll with Rhys Brydydd, Gwilym Tew and Dafydd Benwyn to name just a few.

The pre-industrial hilltop hamlet of Bleanau, evolved from Celtic Saints of the 6th Century, around the time of St. David, our Patron Saint.

Top Llan (as it is locally known) contains of 2 ancient public houses. Corner House at one time spanned 3 cottages which were built in 1722. It was an old Tithe Barn and later a school.

Old House is also an Inn, but from an earlier period in time. It is a thatched establishment called Yr Hen Dy (Old House) and is reputedly the oldest Inn throughout South Wales.

The well known tradition of the Mari Lwyd (Grey Mare) was a fascinating custom during ancient times. It involved a group of people dressed in colourful clothing, with the scary horse's scull draped in a white sheet. They would travel from house to house demanding food and refreshment. This macabre custom is now sunk into the history books, although a more modern and friendly custom is still practiced in Llangynwd today.

Llangynwd is probably most famous for its legendary tale of the Maid of Cefn Ydfa, Ann Thomas. Will Hopcyn, a bard, thatcher and poet was devoted to her in an ill-fated love story. Ann, an heiress to a wealthy farming family, was forbidden to see Will as her mother had branded him to be too poor. Ann was locked in her bedroom and prohibited to contact her only love Will. But secretly, Ann wrote letters to him using her own blood and gave them to a servant to place in the hollow of a sycamore tree nearby for him to collect. Heartbroken at being denied contact with Ann, Will moved away to Bristol to work. But, later in time, he had a dream that she was pining for him and hastily returned to Llangynwd only to find her on her deathbed. She had been forced to marry Anthony Maddocks, whom she had never loved. Will visited her and as she reached out to hold him in joy, she tragically died holding his hand as if waiting to see him before the inevitable happened. Ann was buried within the Church and a few years later, Wil Hopcyn' s remains were buried beneath the Yew tree close to the Church porch. They were united at last in death.

The spectral figure of a young lady dressed in black dashes between the trees on the hilltop at Llangynwd, apparently accompanied by an older female wearing a white cloak. Could these images be connected to each other or just illusory phantoms lost in the midst of time?

The Church itself seems to be the home of a ghostly lady wearing a long black dress. She seems to sit on a particular pew chanting the names of the living that are doomed to die in the coming year. But who could this lady be and why does she have an obsession with death in such an alarming way?

The frightful enactment of a white horse galloping up the main road before leaping over a hedgerow has been witnessed. Said to appear on moonlit nights, this mysterious creature performs this deed in silence.

Maesteg

Maesteg was originally a rural village, dating back around 4,000 years, where an Iron Age castle amongst the hills was identified, as well as evidence of Bronze Age settlements.

This small village began to expand during the Industrial Revolution during the early 19th Century.

In 1820s the Iron Works opened, giving trade to local people from the village and beyond. Soon afterwards, Coal Seams also gave further employment within the community.

The Grade II listed Maesteg Town Hall is a prominent feature in the extended town. It was built in 1880, with C R M Talbot MP laying its first foundation stone on 31st October 1880. He had kindly contributed £500.00 towards the construction of the project. With true community spirit riding high, the local miners all agreed to donate one day's wages towards its completion, the total amount exceeding £5,000.00. The hall itself would have a 650 seating capacity. It was designed by Henry Harris, who was a Cardiff resident and his plan began with the building's frontage, which he drafted in Queen Anne style. The entrance would contain a double front of steps to reach the grandeur of the entire building where no expense was spared. It was proposed to host concerts, plays, operas, public meetings and other forms of entertainment for the public to enjoy.

Unfortunately, the hall underwent refurbishments between 1913 and 14 and the structure's outer appearance lost the majority of its original character. It was reopened on 25th November 1914 to a rousing performance by Nantyffullon Harmonic Society. The ornate tower, (known as the clock tower) was the centerpiece of the town and visible from all corners of the community.

With closure looming and the threat of the demise of such an iconic landmark, in June 1998 Maesteg Town Hall Ltd took over the running of the hall from Bridgend Council. The saved hall would now remain a focal point for entertainment to accommodate the public for future performances, with pillars above the town observing all activity below it. Its clock faces are visible from all angles of the region, as if watching peoples' activity throughout time and pillars above the town observing all activity below it.

Legend maintains that fairies from Ireland dance around the hills above the town, living in a mysterious but warped tree. Wherever this tree stands upon the hillside, it is said to be unlucky to raise deadwood from beneath it. With its tales of folklore breathing down upon us below, would any wise man want to break a tradition passed down through the depths of time?

The spectral, but eerie image of a giant pack of wolves have been reported to stalk the hills overlooking the town, waiting in the darkness to pounce on unsuspecting victims. Why would these fearful creatures want to roam an area beyond their natural habitat, lost in the midst of time?

The ghostly figure of a man has been seen by staff, roaming around the Town Hall. He seems to answer to the name George, but who this gentleman was during his time on the earth and why would he want to linger around a place that he would no longer recognise?

Eerie happenings within the clock tower affect the mechanism in mysterious ways. Photographs have identified strange etchings reading L/cpl Biggins, Blaydon on Tyne, 2/101943 – 9/2/1944. George Biggins had actually carved out his name in the tower before being sent to the Normandy Landings. Could the ghostly apparition who roams the building be George who survived the war and passed away in 1973, reminding bystanders of his human existence in the area?

Merthyr Mawr

The unique village of Merthyr Mawr lies 2½ miles southwest of Bridgend. It is an intriguing beauty spot with pasture lands on the lower valley of the River Ogmore. With its traditional thatched cottages overlooking the village green, it gives a dreamy example of an idyllic settlement itching to remind us of its ancient past.

On the outskirts of Merthyr Mawr is the iconic Grade II listed New Bridge, a single tracked humped overpass made of dressed stone with 4 arches and parapets. It replaced a wooden deck on stone piers prior to the early 19th Century structure. A plaque is set in the wall bearing the inscription *'This Bridge was built at the expence of Right Honourable Sir John Nicholl under the inspection of William County Surveyor by Morgan Thomas of Laleston 1827.'*

Sir John Nicholl had obtained the Merthyr Mawr Estate in 1804, building himself a large house, a new road into the village and a bridge to carry stagecoaches across the water, replacing the old ford. Also known as the 'Dipping Bridge' it was used by local farmers to push reluctant sheep into the water for their annual dip.

The legendary New Inn relates to Cap Coch, an evil man who wore a red cap as a tribute to the French Freedom Fighters. He enticed weary travellers to his Inn, which stood in a hollow on the track road from Bridgend beside the River Ogmore. Most ill-fated travellers were known as packmen, often on horseback or in horse-drawn carriages and would carry valuable products such as wool, skins, stockings and flannel, who were often just single tradesmen in need of refreshment at the Inn. Together with outlaws and smugglers, Cap Coch would murder his rich victims in order to become wealthy by stealing their wares and taking them to market to sell. The truth of these immoral deeds came to light with the discovery of countless bodies buried around the area of the ruinous and later demolished Inn.

The eye-catching Church of St. Teilo is at the heart of the village and became Grade II listed in 1963. This gothic style building was constructed during 19th Century on the site of a 14th Century ancient Church. St. Teilo was the grandson of King Ceredig of Ceredigion and was born around 500 AD. He was considered to be the most Holy man in Wales as he worked and travelled with St. David, the patron Saint of Wales.

Stones of interest relating to the era of Paulinus include the wheel-cross and large sandstone slab with the inscription *'Here lies those Baudewin and his wife Lycia. God rest their souls in peace. Amen'* are significant reminders of the people who dwelt here in the past. A 16th Century map refers to Baudwins's House which was positioned southwest of Merthyr Mawr.

The sand dunes (also known as Merthyr Mawr Warren) span a large area and consist of blown sand. Once thought to be the largest sand dune complex in Europe, they stretch along the coastline to Mumbles. Because of its golden sands extending over a vast section of the shoreline, parts of the Hollywood film 'Lawrence of Arabia' were filmed in the area. One particular dune is named 'The Big Dipper' as it is thought to be the highest in Europe.

Although a daunting challenge, archaeologists found items from our Prehistoric past as well as the Neolithic Age, with findings such as flint tools, arrowheads, knives, scrapers and stone workings. Bronze Age items dating from 400-300 BC were also unearthed. Early Iron Age objects were also uncovered including bronze crucibles, brooches and pins. Other interesting finds from all walks of life include a sand mound amid covered stones with 6 burial plots, 2 of which were in cists. The Skeletons of 2 men buried in vessels were also found. A mysterious building also stood in a ruinous state on the sand hills, which was thought to be the remains of a Celtic windmill. These Celtic-speaking people are thought to have travelled from Somerset.

The phantom image of a wagon pulled by 3 horses has been seen on a number of occasions tearing through the village at pace. Locals claim that seeing this apparition is considered bad luck as the 'special taper' (or corpse candle) eerily guides the eye towards the apparition of the wagon. But could this ghostly parade be from an era when a freak thunderstorm struck and the horse, driver and coach were swept into the swollen river, never to be seen again?

The frightful feeling of being watched by unseen eyes around the entrance to the sand hills often overcomes peoples' emotions, only for them to discover that no physical person is actually there. Could the ghosts of the past be keeping a watchful eye over their patch from an era beyond our grasp?

Candleston Castle

The fortified Manor House known as Candleston Castle dates back to the 14th Century and can be found on the edge of Merthyr Mawr sand dunes. The original structure was long and narrow in rectangular shape. But over the years it had been extended including a West wing which was added during 17th Century. Occupation of this once glorious abode is rather vague. But it is believed to have been built by the Norman-Welsh Catilupe family, which is where Candleston adopted its name from, although no actual records exist of this particular family ever living there.

It was during the 19th Century that Candleston Castle/Manor House was abandoned and has been left to ruin ever since, becoming just a shadow of its former self with only nature for company.

Remaining original features of this once magnificent

structure consist of a polygonal courtyard and 2m high wall. Although, some parts of the remaining edifice have more recently been repaired, including the large fireplace, the West wall window and the Southern end of the tower elevated.

Many old buildings and structures do seem to have a reputation for myths, legends and ghostly beings from times gone by, as they seemingly attach themselves to the fabric of a place they once called home.

Candleston Castle is thought to have been built within a lost village called Treganlaw, meaning town of a hundred hands. The village is believed to have been buried under the sand dunes of Merthyr Mawr after a frightful storm. Who knows if this legend is to be believed or if it is an old wives tale passed down through the generations.

The stillness of this derelict structure can send shivers down the spine with its chilling emptiness. But ghostly beings still tend to hold onto their place of residence with stones and crosses thrown by unseen hands. One stone is fittingly called the Goblin Stone which seems to entice the innocent to embrace it by trapping their hands and feet amongst the scattered ancient carvings, with only a prayer to disentangle them. The stone is said to hold vibrations of paranormal activity with invisible hands drawing onlookers towards it. Is this ghostly fable fact or fiction and who would be brave enough to enter into a world of the unknown? Could it be you observing these unusual happenings?

North Cornelly

Cornelly was originally a sub village to the Borough of Kenfig. It is thought to be named after the Breton Saint Cornelius, but is more likely to have embraced the De Cornelly family name as its beginnings who adopted the surname when they lived in the southern village at Ty Maen in the ancient Manor House.

North Cornelly, however, was first documented in 1183 and was known as 'The Vill of Walter Lupellus' by distinct crossroads where the original village branched off from the main road. Lupelluston was then adopted as the village name in the early 13th Century and was possibly from the Anglo-Normans meaning 'wolf cub'.

The 700 year old crossroads was known as Croes y Green. They were originally thought to have been on the road towards the village of Maudlam, although this ancient landmark is now lost in time as it is buried beneath the raging sands of the dunes to the Southeast of North Cornelly. Croes y Green was the 13th Century main point enroute between the Cardiff and Kenfig highway and was where Heol y Sheet and Heol Las were the heart of the area. It was connected to the ancient track leading to towns and villages more far afield, with documents from the medieval period stating that this track began from Stormy Down.

Croes y Green was a public meeting place where toll-gates were operated. Also known as turnpikes, these were small gateways or pikes that would turn to allow horses and carriages through to continue their journey. Payment for using the toll was essential otherwise access through would be denied, forcing journeymen to advance over the rougher landscape if they were unable to pay the levy.

The crossroads were forced more inland later in time because of the advancing sand from the dunes which buried the main highway. The toll-gate at the crossroads was also a gathering place for folk to resolve disputes during the unsettling period of 1843.

The original village of North Cornelly lay a relatively long distance from Croes y Green, close to the village of Maudlam. But when it was relocated, the crossroads were set between the Manor House (Hall Farm) and the New

30

House Inn.

On North Cornelly Cross, a Blacksmith's shop was opened in 1738 and continued to trade until as recent as the 20th Century. There were also three public houses listed within this area: The Old House Inn, Cornelly Arms and New House Inn, although the Old House was demolished years ago and the others ceased trading more recently.

Other major street names included Old School Road and Heol Fach (little Road). Carbide Works were also a main place of employment for villagers nearby.

New House Inn was once a Malt House which brewed its own beer with a butcher's shop occupying part of the building. An old cottage with a thatched roof was situated behind and was inhabited by the Edwards family where one member eventually purchased the Inn.

Legend maintains that a sour-faced lady wearing a red hooded cloak, riding a black steed and surrounded by fearful hounds has been witnessed. She was nicknamed 'Mallt y Nos' by terrified villagers as she was deemed to disperse evil amongst the community. Her appearance along the misty terrain usually happened around the time of the hunting season.

The alarming sight of large black cats stalking the wilderness sends fear amongst witnesses. It is possible that these outsized animals were exotic pets such as panthers and pumas which were left to roam after being abandoned following the popular fashion accessory during the 1960s and 1970s. Their appearance has been known to scare people into retreat as they seem to don glittery collars whilst parading around the area. Could these be the local legends of ABCs (Alien Black Cats), siblings of abnormal pets, or mass fabrication?

Another fable of hell-hounds involves these frightful beasts prowling in large quantities seemingly on the hunt for victims around the crossroads. Pitiful howls have also been heard bellowing out across the land, with their piercing red eyes of evil glaring towards the innocent. Also known as Cwn Annwn, or Gwyllgi its ancient equivalent, these large creatures are said to cast curses of sickness and death amongst communities if seen in packs. If their master on horseback is seen in the same spectral vision, the death of a loved one is said to be the prediction.

Ogmore Castle

Established by William de Londres in 1116, the first castle on the site was constructed using earth and timber. This was around the time of the Norman invasion and eventually the castle and additional keep were built using stone for strength against enemy attack.

The inner ward can still be seen as well as the great tower which was built by Maurice de Londres, son of William, after his father's death in 1126. It was likely to have been a spectacular sight as it spanned 3 stories with a fireplace on the ground floor. Staircases for the first floor were added for apartments to accommodate the Lord and his family. Across from the main castle another building was added during the 12th Century, although only ruins of the cellar remain today.

The de Londres family still owned the castle during the 13th Century and they added more new buildings to the site where the foundations are still visible. Buildings which probably stood on the site include a gatehouse and a great hall block. Indications of an original drawbridge are still evident beside the gate passage. However, the castle is unlikely to have served against any substantial battles.

Other significant names relating to the castle include Payn de Chaworth, Lord of Kidwelly and his heiress Matilda who married Henry, Earl of Lancaster in 1298. Ogmore castle then became part of the Duchy of Lancaster in England and served as a courthouse during the 14th Century.

The ghostly, but lifelike, image of a man has been seen on many occasions by unsuspecting visitors, walking across the stepping stones seemingly looking for hidden treasure within the castle. He had been informed about the lost treasure by the Lady of Ogmore and died of an illness shortly afterwards. He eerily haunts the entire area guarding the loot, unaware that his prize had disappeared years ago.

Another phantom entity has been seen crossing the water displaying himself as a soldier from a distant era. Could this gallantry spirit be guarding Lady of Ogmore during his time on the earth?

The spectral image of a local poacher has been identified roaming around the castle grounds. Could this frightful image be a figment of imagination, or that of a poacher executed on the land many years ago reluctant to leave the place where he met his end?

Pencoed

The town of Pencoed, or Pencoyd as it is pronounced in English, is situated to the northeast of Bridgend and has expanded over the years. It has adjusted to lying within 3 districts which increased to four hamlets: Penprysg (corpse end), Cefn Hirgoed (long wood ridge), Hendre (old settlement) and Felindre (mill settlement). There is evidence that Pencoed was at one time occupied during the Neolithic/Bronze Age era, as flint flakes and teeth from plentiful animals have been found. Hendre is the oldest settlement as it looks out towards the common land called Ystradwaun.

Although locals call it Pencawd or Pencode, it was during the 19th Century that the population increased when the coal mines became a major part of employment, but were closed when coal became less of a necessity.

The original town was built on a Norman castle with various streams rising and running through the area. The two main rivers Ewenny Fawr (great river) and Ewenny Fach (little river) are widely associated with its decent toward Ogmore by Sea where it runs into the Bristol Channel.

Pencoed railway is a minor station which is located in the square above the War Memorial (or the Monument as locals refer to it) and was opened in June 1850. It became another casualty of the Dr. Beeching cuts and railway closures in 1964. It reopened again on 11th May 1992 with two platforms.

As with most towns and villages throughout Wales, Pencoed is not immune to tales of ghosts, myths and legends:

The eerie sight of a horse-drawn carriage careering at speed from an invisible side road with just a lantern shining at the front for light, has been seen on a number of occasions, only to disappear in an instant. Does the driver of this coach not understand that his time on earth is now misplaced in a modern town and his invisible track road?

Witnessed at night, the spectral image of a lady with long tangled hair and wearing what appears to be a long white dress has been seen standing in the road, only to vanish into thin air. As the road was grassland before our time, could this ghostly apparition be oblivious to our modern world and seemingly intent on taunting the living?

As I have connections with Pencoed through my grandfather, who was born in the town and told me much about its history, it was captivating when he told the story of my ancestor Megan who was convicted of witchcraft and burnt at the stake on the Common Centuries ago. She was in reality the more innocent white witch who made herbal remedies to cure sick animals, which is not in any form delving into the more sinister black arts. This barbaric practice was administered during the 16th and 17th Centuries and I believe that my ancestor was in the latter. There were 5 witches executed for their supposed crimes in Wales between 1655 and 1684, so Megan would have been condemned between those dates.

Built on the site of an old farmhouse within the area of Pencoed, one house, in particular, experiences lively ghostly happenings occurring with cups exploding for no apparent reason and electrical equipment turning itself on and off by unseen hands. Could a ghostly farmer from times gone by be uneasy about modern gadgets and thrusting poltergeist activity to scare the living?

Porthcawl

The name Porthcawl dates as far back as 1628 from a survey of Pembroke Manor and was called Port Call. In 1825, an Act of Parliament referred to the area as Pwll

Cawl Bay. It was primarily developed during the Victorian era as a town and holiday destination, which had previously been occupied by agricultural industries.

James and Mary Caroline Brogden, lived in Seabank House on the seafront from around 1865. It later became a school and then a hotel. They were important figures throughout the town and were responsible for many of the buildings throughout Porthcawl, leaving reminders of their existence with street names. Mary Street was associated with Mary Caroline and John Street was named after James' father John, who was the head of the family firm called John Brogden & Sons of Sale. Some of the original features of these elegant buildings built by the Brogden family are still visible throughout John Street today, although many have sadly been demolished.

The town centre (John Street) has been a fashionable shopping area since the early 1900s, which is when most of the buildings were completed. The town centre was always decorated during the Christmas season with many differing ornamentation throughout time, including the lighting of candles, which in today's modern world would be deemed dangerous.

Porthcawl was also known for its shipping, dockyard and railway during that era, which attracted many workers of all trades to settle in the area. Public Houses, Guest Houses and Hotels became very popular as Porthcawl and its surrounding villages seemed to entice tourists and workers alike, making this glorious town a booming destination for holiday seekers.

With such a vibrant amount of movement from differing eras, would the ghostly beings of yesteryear be lurking in the background silently observing the people of today in a township that they would no longer recognize?

At the dead of night when the roads are quiet, the strange sound of marching has been heard. It has been described as hearing an invisible army parading through the street; yet no physical bodies are seen. Could these eerie sounds be a re-enactment of the soldiers from both World Wars who proudly marched through the town at the end of conflict, or just a misjudged hallucination?

The well known legend of the Mari Lwyd (a horse's skull on a pole and carried by a person hidden under a sackcloth) during the Christmas period was a fascinating tradition for many years during ancient times. It originally demonstrated the Nativity scene with a parade of people dressed in colourful clothing, three of whom were Mary, Joseph and the baby Jesus. This folklore was later replaced by a scarier scene. It included a man dressed with a white cotton sheet shrouding his body and the skull of a horse over his head. He would be accompanied by the leader, the sergeant and Punch and Judy puppets and their aim would be to spread fear in the form of the 'grey mare' at Christmas. The skull dowsed in ribbons, glass eyes in its sockets with a lantern inside to add to a terrifying effect, they would perform throughout the streets of towns and villages and demand entry into innocent people's houses asking for hospitality with food and drink, cascading fear into the occupants of the house. This frightful parade probably did occur around the town of Porthcawl during those ancient times of darkness.

Thankfully, this tradition is now a distant memory, as it caused outrage and was deemed an invasion of privacy.

Porthcawl Lighthouse

The coastline of Porthcawl has been the subject of news over the past decades with the devastating storms that have battered its shores with some catastrophic incidents. Two cannons were churned up by the raging sea and are on show in the Porthcawl Museum in John Street. They are believed to be from an 18th Century ship.

A new lighthouse (goleudy in Welsh) at Porthcawl Point, at the Eastern entrance to Swansea Bay and in the Bristol Channel, was built in 1866 by Messrs Stephen of Bristol. The intention was to deter vessels from the treacherous rocks around the shore, as many ships had been lost to the sea in this particular area in days gone by. It was constructed using cast-iron, painted in black and white and built on a hexagonal stone base, whilst set upon a rectangular plinth behind an outer sea wall.

The tower tapers and has small vents bolted midway up each side. It had a hinged metal door with a handle and catches for safety for its keepers against the stormy weather battering the coast with violent waves roaring over the structure.

In 1840 the main breakwater was extended by 100 yards, prior to the lighthouse being built. The lantern (powered by gas) and the top were replaced with a domed cap and a small round finial with curved bolted frames and glazed panels after another severe storm in 1996 where the metal ladder was ingested up by the raging tide.

According to 1871 census the first Lighthouse man at Porthcawl Lighthouse was John Pervis, a 72 year old man born in Cardigan. Coastguards listed at that time were Timothy Kelly, (34) from Cork and Whilfield Martin (37) from Minehead. They all lived on New Road, a popular domain for workers throughout the town of Porthcawl.

In 1911 a severe storm damaged the lighthouse and the pyramidal roof with its weathervane and lantern had to be replaced. It was powered by gas from the gas works in New Road until 1974, when North Sea gas took over the mission of keeping vulnerable ships informed of the dangers around the coast.

Porthcawl Lighthouse on the Breakwater at Porthcawl Harbour became Grade II listed in August 1991.

Other listed monuments around this area of Porthcawl include the Outer Basin, the Breakwater, the Look-Out Tower, the Old Customs House and Jennings Warehouse.

As with many coastal areas around Wales, Porthcawl does seem to have its own share of ghostly tales:

The chilling image of a man wearing what appears to be a trilby hat and dark overcoat seems to stand on the pier smoking a pipe. He then disappears in a shimmering haze. Who could this man in old fashioned dress be and is he trapped between reality and beyond?

The alarming sound of an outmoded fog bell has been heard at the dead of night bellowing out across the sea. Could this illusory sound be warning modern vessels that danger lurks beneath the perilous tides?

The hazy figure of an old-fashioned mariner has been spotted, appearing to float around the body of the lighthouse. Could this unusual image be a sailor from a vulnerable ship lost in the depths of the perilous sea from days gone by?

Mysterious but large footprints have been discovered on the path leading to the lighthouse; followed by a loud bang piercing the ears of passersby, yet no physical person is seen to be performing any of these routines. With a flash of light coming from the lighthouse, both footprints and eerie sounds vanish. Could this be from a keeper from our past reminding us of the drudgery of his working life?

After the ferociousness of winter, on misty mornings in March, the hazy image of a stricken ship can be seen around the coast of Porthcawl. Said to resemble a galleon, this creepy ship only appears every ten years. Perhaps this disturbing image is making the living aware of its fate on the anniversary of its sinking.

Porthcawl Museum

The Old Police Station, now Porthcawl Museum and other organisations such as the Art Society, is a two storey building with six gabled bays with narrow attic openings paired to the right. It was built by John Pritchard, a Diocesan Architect from Llandaff who designed many other structures in the area.

Its purpose was to keep law and order within the town of Newton Nottage (as it was known at the time) and consisted of a gaol, Superintendent's house and prisoners yard to the rear. According to Buildings of Wales documentation, the Old Police Station was built in 1877 and remained in use until 1973. It was awarded a Grade II listing in 1989 by CADW.

The first floor of the edifice's frontage has sash windows, all with relieving arches. The main station itself was to the left with a central shouldered doorway beside a sash window with lintel and original lettering, whereas to the right the Superintendent's house could be located. This, at the time, was visually separated from the main Police Station by a deeply recessed pointed arched entrance of two orders with spur bases. The doors were boarded with strapwork hinges as a safeguard against prisoner escape.

I had the pleasure of interviewing Mair Harrys who informed me that during World War II behind the Old Police Station was a Fire Station as she often drove the fire engine in emergencies as the majority of local men were required to engage in combat.

The building's design is in typical Tudorbethan style, which was popular during that time and was decked with modern features with rock faced stone, coursed to the left and snecked to the right with ashlar dressings; slate roof with terracotta ridge tiles and large blue brick chimney stacks with octagonal flues was a fashionable style for this type of building back then.

The Museum was closed for refurbishment in 1997 and the gaol was reported to be largely intact with a whitewashed bricked corridor and three cells, with small pane windows and round arched bricked vaulted ceilings. For security the cells were boarded and doors studded for the protection of the innocent.

Due to its age and location in such a busy town throughout time, it would be inevitable that Porthcawl Museum attracts visitors of the supernatural kind.

The chilling echo of a ghostly being treading the boards of the upper floors wearing what sounds like heavy rubber-soled boots has been heard on a few occasions. Could this be a manifestation of the activities of the building's working past, haunting the present?

In the upper gallery, the eerie appearance of a middle-aged man wearing Victorian dress has been reported to walk along its floors only to vanish into thin air. Who could this old-fashioned gentleman be and what entices him to revisit a building which has changed over time?

The sight of a flickering phantom lantern has been seen, seemingly floating in mid air around the entrance corridor before disappearing at the blink of an eye; yet no person seems to be accompanying its ghostly appearance. Could the wardens of yesteryear be guiding the living through the darkness of time, or just illusion of time?

New Road itself was constructed as a building development in 1862 under the supervision of the Reverend Edward Dodderidge Knight, who was the Lord of Pembroke Manor from 1857. He then granted the land to Robert Floyd, father-in-law to W. J. Griffin, who proceeded to build dwellings and other establishments along the site.

New Road at the end of the 19th century accommodated a Gas Works and eleven public houses: the Carpenters Arms which once became a florist shop, the Masons Arms which was once a shop and then a Post Office, now a house, the White Lion which adjoined the shop, the Greyhound on the corner of Mackworth Road, which stood empty for many years before being converted into a cottage, the Mackworth Inn which became a cottage, the Brogden Hotel, Albion Inn which is now called Albion Cottage, the Queens Hotel, the General Picton and The Prince of Wales.

Although New Road was constructed as a building development and containing at least 11 public houses towards the end of the 19th Century, there are also other features which live in history throughout this lengthy road.

Griffin Park is situated opposite the General Picton public house and was at one time the site of allotments purchased by James Brogden from John Sanderson Hollyer and Dame Price.

The Park itself acquired its name from Mr. W. J. Griffin, who purchased the land from the Great Western Railway Company in 1930. As he was a Councillor and Head Teacher at New Road School, the plans for the development were drawn up in the same year by Tudor Morgan, licensee at the General Picton public house and father of Mair Harrys.

The tranquility of the park is mirrored by it bowling greens, tennis courts, beautiful gardens, pavillion and children's playground. Benches were also erected on the opposite side, for people to freely idle away their time and admire the magnificent park. Mr. Griffin lived parallel to the park so that he could enjoy the pleasure of observing people's delight at the newly created leisure estate.

New Road also had many individual trades, including toy shops, a general store (Richard Sampsons), grocery suppliers, sweet shops and shoe stores. Residential housing within the road gave its occupiers employment such as in schooling, coal, masonry, various mills, agriculture, tourism, shipping, the dockyard and the railways.

Ghostly Tales of New Road

New Road seems to attract ghostly beings on an unexpected scale, as the tales of time have stated. It is said that these images have a tendency to prowl this lengthy road at the dead of night.

A phantom gathering of men in old fashioned clothing seem to gather on the corner opposite the school, mainly on winter evenings. Could this unlikely group be waiting for their daily drink from a long gone public house, or just a mass figment of imagination?

The spectral image of a soldier has been seen by unsuspecting bystanders, loiterng on street corners. It is not know who he was, but why would such a gallantry serviceman want to return to a time of conflict and sadness?

The ghostly sight of a young girl dressed in a white shift has been seen on a number of occasions, happily skipping up an imaginary road, only to disappear into thin air. Could this child be Elizabeth whom the Porthcawl Paranormal Team had come into contact with during an investigation at the General Picton in 2006, who had tragically drowned in Saint David's well, or just another unfortunate child whose life was cruelly snatched from beneath her?

THE DEVIL SAID

I WILL BE , WHAT EVER YOU WANT ME TO BE

I WILL BE KIND, IF IT SUITS YOU, OR UNKIND
WHICH WILL SUITE ME

I WILL WALK THROUGH THE CORRIDORS OF
YOURMIND AND OPEN DOORS THAT YOU HAVE
LOCKED FOR I HOLD THE KEYS

TO BELIEVE IN ME, YOU WILL ENJOY THE
CHAOS THAT WILL BE YOUR LIFE

JEALOUSY, HATE, REVENGE WILL INFECT,
LIKE AN ILLNESS, WHICH WILL POLLUTE THE
WEAK AND

VULNERABLE WHO ARE MY FOLLOWING,
WHO, WILL OBTAIN GREATNESS WITH MY
GUIDANCE AS HISTORY HAS PROVED

EVEN AT MY DEFEAT AT ARMAGEDDON THE
DEAD ARE MY VICTORY.

ALL MEN ARE BORN IMPERFECT... THERE LIES
MY RESURRECTION?

By Peter Stallard

The Rest Convalescent Home

Rest Bay is a popular parcel of land in Porthcawl and lies to the east of the town. Upon the hillside, overlooking the coast, is a dominant building appropriately named The Rest, which became a Grade II listed building in 1998. It was awarded this status because it contributes towards our South Wales industrial history and is credited with being the work of 3 of Wales' most distinguished architects whose intention it was to create a convalescent home for recuperation.

The main building was the brainchild of architect John Pritchard who began its construction in 1874, although plans had been drawn up in 1869. The site itself had been donated by the Talbot family of Margam to create a suitable building for workers of the mines and collieries from surrounding areas. The left wing and water tower were added in 1891 by G F Lambert, the rear left wing in 1900 and the right wing in 1909 by E M Bruce Vaughan. It is thought that 2 cottages in New Road were used prior to the building of The Rest which accommodated workers in 1862, courtesy of the infamous Brogden family. These were designated following the cholera outbreak of 1849 in the Bridgend and Cowbridge districts.

The Rest Home had 50 fireplaces positioned appropriately throughout the building for necessary heat, as well as a good ventilation system. The building's original design housed male and female separate blocks which were built by Gorvetts of Bristol. The modern home for its era opened in 1877 with its first patients who were survivors of the Ty Newydd Colliery disaster, a tragedy which occurred on 11th April that year. Funding for the project was obtained from subscriptions leading right up to 1960s. The aim was to give sympathy to the poorer families of our community who could not afford the luxuries of healthcare.

As the main building was used to accommodate men

46

only, the left wing extension was added in 1891 to accommodate women. The final extension in 1900 provided a refuge for children with treatments including hot and cold sea-water baths.

According to the 1881 census, Ann Hughes (a widow aged 73) was the matron overseeing the cleanliness and smooth running of the establishment, whereas in 1891 George Evans was its manager.

On 3rd January 1890 a performance was staged at the Bridgend Town Hall and all profits were donated to the Rest Convalescent Home as an outbreak of bronchial flu had gripped the nation. Miss Jones from the nearby Clevedon House School was called upon to vaccinate all patients.

During the two World Wars the Rest Home was used as an auxiliary hospital for wounded soldiers. In World War II planes were commanded to operate on the grassland known as Lock's Common, which is close the Rest Home and an ideal location for recuperation.

The Rest Home was built on a large scale and dominates the skyline. It was built using cuff and rock faced sandstone in chalet-type style with a first floor balcony. The roof was dressed using Welsh slate. Sadly the building was sold to be transformed into more modern accommodation.

Because of its location facing the sea and its prominence in history, it would seem inevitable that tales of paranormal phenomena have taken a grip on this picturesque area.

A standing stone close to the Rest Home is rumoured to have connections with Elizabeth, The Maid of Sker. She is a famous ghostly being attached to Sker House, (a short distance from the Rest) who was forbidden by her father to marry her lover; a harpist named Thomas Evans and died of a broken heart after being forced to marry another man.

She is said to have secretly left love tokens buried beneath the stone for her true love. Her spirit has been reported to linger around its base reaching out in devotion, only for no-one to arrive to greet her. Could this Maid be patiently hiding in wait for her only true love, or just an untimely misjudgment of the mind?

On the distant seas towards Sker rocks, a ghostly ship has been seen mirroring white mist around it, particularly on stormy nights, when the Church bells will distinctly ring out. Could these scary happenings be a re-enactment of a ship lost to the treacherous seas when bells would ring out warning its people of disaster?

The Rest Home itself is no stranger to the ghostly visions of the lifelike image of a man dressed in black old fashioned clothing. He is said to roam the corridors, particularly at the dead of night. But who could this gentleman be and is he determined to remain around a place that he once adored?

The phantom figure of a man wearing a trench coat has been witnessed prowling the vast grounds surrounding the Rest. He seems to wander the area in silence before disappearing in a hazy mist. Could this be the soul of a soldier who spent time within the building during the perils of such a tragic war?

A portly lady wearing a white apron and wielding a knife was often witnessed by staff around the area of the kitchen, giving them a fright. Who could this intimidating lady be and why does she seem so intent on displaying this chilling image?

Pen-y-Fai

The village of Penyfai (also known as Pen-y-Vai) lies within the borough of Bridgend and has a population of around 2000 residents in our modern era. The village itself from a bygone age belonged to the Court Coleman Estate, which was built in 1776 with a Manor House erected for the Llewellyn family who dwelt there for many years. In fact, documents from 1837 assert that the Estate was owned by Colonel Llewellyn. It had become a Gentleman's residence around this time and had been renovated and extended throughout the generations of the family until it was sold in 1960. A smaller house named White Hall was then built behind the large Church. Court Coleman Manor was subsequently converted to accommodate guests as a hotel appropriately called Court Coleman.

The Parish place of worship, named The Church of All Saints, is a prominent feature of the village and is Grade II listed along with the Church Lodge and School Lodge. These three were built between 1898 and 1903 by Robert W Llewellyn from Court Coleman Manor. This was because these buildings were at one time the entrance to the Court Coleman Estate. Robert Llewellyn was a member of the Baglan family, who gifted many Churches to the County. The Church of All Saints is a cruciform erection and local stone from the quarry was used for its creation with a tower at its centre containing 5 bells. The Churchyard has an ancient cross, which was discovered within the walls of a farmhouse in 1930. It represents St. Leonard in chains from 17/18 Century.

During the construction of the main road through Pen-y-Fai, fragments of ancient pottery were found together with coins, giving us a broader insight into the origins of this sleepy village.

To the South of Pen-y-Fai village are two ancient wells; and to the North large masses of outcrop rocks which have been documented as prehistoric monolithe.

The Tyn-y-garn Mile Marker (or Milepost) in Penycae

Lane is also Grade II listed and dates back to Victorian times. It has links with the South Wales Railway and displays the distance of 2½ miles to the main station in Bridgend.

Another Grade II listed structure is the Glan Rhyd Railway Viaduct which overpasses the River Ogmore. It dates back to our Industrial past and a plaque with the engraving '*This bridge was erected in the year 1829 by Morgan Thomas, Laleston, Mason*' nearby as a reminder of the toils of yesteryear.

The Pheasant public house is on the South side of Pen-y-Fai and is also Grade II listed. It was originally a medieval hall, parlour house and farmhouse in the 15th Century. It was also home to the Welsh Baptist Chapel before being converted into a public house in 1967. The quarry to its rear provided stone for building structures within the locality.

Pen-y-Fai is also home to the only Dogs Trust in Wales and serves the community well.

With such a varied history throughout the years, Pen-y-Fai does seem to attract visitors of the supernatural kind.

The startling apparitions of two people dressed in white clothing appearing to hold hands seem to wander towards the milepost. Their shimmering bodies rapidly fade into the distance and vanish in an extraordinary fashion. But who could this couple be and are they waiting for transport that will never arrive?

On rain-swept nights the silhouettes of a man, woman and child appear around the area of Court Coleman. These figures seem intent on making their presence known by staring at bystanders in an impish way before vanishing through a solid wall. Could this family have been residents of Court Coleman during the days of our past, desperate to guard their former abode?

The viaduct stands tall amongst its surroundings and paints an empty picture of a once busy railway line. The ghostly noise of an invisible train possibly does not recognise that locomotives ceased travelling along this track long ago.

The eerie sound of this ghost train has been heard on many occasions, chuffing along aimlessly towards its now evaporated destination. It is considered by locals to be lucky to hear the ghost train travelling along this awesome line, a superstition which many still believe today. One person alarmingly caught a glimpse of a phantom train, only for it to disappear at the blink of an eye. Do the spirits of yesteryear still dwell on their hard labour by retracing the journey to what they believed to be occupational hardship?

The terrifying feeling of being followed by an unearthly person trailing behind the living whilst walking around the milepost has been felt, only for victims to realise that no physical person is there. Why would a spiritual entity want to prey on innocent victims from a world beyond their understanding?

Pyle

The small community of Pyle (or Y Pîl in Welsh) lies 6 miles west of Bridgend and is served by the A48 clearway. It is mainly recognised by its crossroads at the heart of the vicinity.

Directly off the crossroads is the impressive St. James' Church which towers above the community, replacing the lost Church of Kenfig prior to 1485. It therefore adopted the same name by an order from the diocesan court by the people of Pyle. It was built in perpendicular style with a castellated tower, chancel, nave and south porch to name but a few distinct features. But during ancient times the original priest's door leading into the chancel was walled in, an action typical of that period. Registers relating to the Church date back to 1695. It is also appropriately styled in similarity to the Church at nearby Maudlam, a small village adjacent to Kenfig. Maybe it was a Church from another village which was rebuilt using the top layer for foundation and the Church's brickwork would become smaller as the tower was built, giving it the label by locals who affectionately know it as *'The Upside Down Church'*.

A 12th Century document states that a ford 'Redesice' (Rhyd y Sais – The English Ford) crossed the Avan Vach around the spot of the modern railway bridge.

During 13th Century most of the land at Pyle and the surrounding area was owned by the Grammas family who may have lived at Marlas, also known as Grammas Hill.

The origins of the community are surrounded by mystery. But during medieval times it fell into the district of Peytevin, which was when Pyle was originally created (1439) because the sands had engulfed the old town of Kenfig and the Burgesses spread throughout the vicinity to take refuge from the raging sandstorms. Pyle was an enroute trail between Stormy Down and Margam and was recognized as a settlement area for the re-establishment of the new town of Kenfig itse.

It was Richard Neville (Warwick the Kingmaker who put 2 kings upon the throne) who attempted to transfer the Borough of Kenfig. Unfortunately he was executed during the Battle of Barnet in 1471, so he did not achieve his goal. However, this date was carved into a shield high in the roof of the nave of the Church in remembrance of him. Could his faithful parishioners have performed this deed as a mark of respect to their knight in shining armour?

Pyle was an important village during the mid 19th Century because of the Industrial Development period in time.

On the A48 clearway towards Margam a large house stands, stretching back from the road. Built by Thomas Mansel Talbot around 1782, it bears an uncanny resemblance to the Old House Inn, which was probably built around the same time.

A Roman milestone was unearthed in the area, giving us an indication of earlier activity throughout Pyle.

Legend maintains that St. James' Churchyard is no stranger to spooky occurrences, with the chilling sound of a ghostly voice chanting the names of parishioners who are doomed to die in the coming year, particularly at the dead of night on Halloween. This spooky occasion is known to unrest the spirits of the deceased who take pleasure in visiting our earthly realm to play havoc with the living. This ghostly voice can also recite in a different tone the names of those who are due to marry in the coming year. Could these unnerving chants be the spirits of the departed vying for the attention of the living, or just natural reverberations from the surrounding area?

'Bwci Bo' is a gnome-like figure said to live in a field known as Puckwall, which is on the edge of the village of Pyle. This mischievous phantom is said to visit farmhouses at the dead of night casting his spell of bad luck upon residents. But is this illusive image a tale of fantasy passed down through the depths of time?

Another story of eeriness involves a standing stone which once stood in a field to the rear of Ty'n y Cellar farm in Ton Kenfig. Tradition states that it would visit the sea at Sker in Porthcawl to take a drink and then return to its original spot in the field. As this was reported to happen on

Christmas morning, bad luck would follow those who dared to interrupt its path.

Pyle Inn was a public house now lost in time. It was run by two gentlemen, father and son, named John Simpson between 1828 and 1886. Ghostly tales have been rife ever since and the image of a mysterious stagecoach with a team of 6 horses galloping at speed with the driver perched on top curse the area, normally during the hours of darkness. This procession is said to disappear into obscurity, never to be seen again in the same night.

Could this surreal procession be from an era when coach and horses were the only mode of transport?

A sad tale states that one stagecoach tragically overturned when it ran into the parapet of a low bridge many years ago. Could this be a re-enactment of a tragic accident, or a just a tale of fantasy?

South Cornelly

South Cornelly is one of two small neighbouring hamlets to the south of Pyle with its stone and lime quarries now lying abandoned and left to nature.

Lime mortar was widely used for building during olden times. But during the mid 20th Century cement became more popular and a cheaper substance to use.

The 'original' village is South Cornelly, which evolved from an Anglo-Norman settlement dating back to the mid 12th Century, is thought to be named after the DeCornelly family who had adopted this surname instead of their original title.

Thomas, son of William, lived in a house thought to have been on the site of a Manor House called Ty Maen, hidden behind high walls en-route through the village.

According to documents from the period, Cornelly was almost named Thomastown, as his father was Lord of the Manor. But this was abandoned for reasons which were never disclosed.

Ty Maen dated back to 1650, with unusual features, including a Priests hole which was a concealed space for Monks to hide from Henry VIII's army after the dissolution of the Monasteries in 1536. This space was discovered in a bedroom behind an old cupboard in the Manor.

Another more likely theory proclaimed that Cornelly acquired its name from a medieval Chapel, thought to have existed within the vicinity and dedicated to a Breton Saint called Cornelius.

Lamb Row (Rhes Yr Oen) was at one time the original street leading from the main road and contained a small ancient Chapel at the foot of the stony outcrop.

A fascinating legend maintains that the Chapel had a secret tunnel leading directly to the Manor House.

The derelict Chapel on the hill was at one stage transformed into a cottage, but sadly now only its ruined remains are left in the garden of a modern-day dwelling.

Over the past two centuries, the back of the hill where the Chapel once stood was quarried away during the limestone, iron and steel industry years.

There were several limestone quarries and kilns around South Cornelly at that time, which provided employment for inhabitants from the surrounding area.

South Cornelly quarry was the largest producer of limestone and supplied Port Talbot Steelworks with sinter (ground limestone).

Quarrying began during the mid 17th century and it was widely mined up until the mid 20th century: although it is now deserted and reserved for wildlife with woodland and pasture areas.

Pant Mawr quarry was locally known as the Blue Lagoon, as it was laden with water and with the sun reflecting upon it, the glistening pool would display a deep blue appearance.

The Dyffryn Llynfi railway was a tram road for horse drawn carriages transporting iron and coal to the Porthcawl dockyard.

In South Cornelly, a lane intersected the railway line when steam trains were introduced in 1861 and manned by a signal box.

The keeper's house survived the Dr. Beeching axe and was subsequently converted into an abode standing opposite the now forgotten Three Horse Shoes public house. This was originally named The Horse and Tram and lay alongside the railway.

The Turpin family settled in Cornelly in the late 18th century, when Captain Richard Turpin (1691-1764) took over Grove Farm on the edge of South Cornelly. When he died, he passed the farm to his sons Francis and John who had links with Newton in Porthcawl. The family are not thought to have had any association with Dick Turpin, the feared highwayman.

Another famous name relating to the village is Mary Francis, who died at the age of 110 in September 1890. She was hailed the 'Cornelly Centenarian' and 'Honary Aunt' by villagers; hence thousands attended her funeral at Maudlam Church.

Flowers to Boppa Francis (her affectionate nickname) mysteriously appear upon her grave, keeping her memory alive, even to this day!

Mary had lived in Chapel Cottage at the side of the railway and close to a Calvinist Methodist Chapel; and even though it is now a ruin, the startling image of a four-poster bed draped in a white sheet with a body beneath it is rumoured to float above the invisible cottage on moonlit nights. Could this be Mary's final moments during her time on earth, vying to be remembered?

In the vicinity of the Kissing Gate, a lady wearing a white dress is alleged to haunt the area. Said to be in search of her baby, she seems to loiter around the invisible gateway waiting for someone to kiss her. This deed would release her sorrow and reunite her with her child. But who could this lady be and why is she waiting for such an unlikely gesture from humankind?

The frightful sight of a portly man falling into the quarry before vanishing into thin air has been witnessed. Who could this gentleman have been during his time on earth and why would he want to terrify the living by recreating such a tragic event.

Stormy Down

This once stretch of open countryside with limestone quarries lies 2 miles south east of Pyle. Its name derives from a Norman family called Sturmi, who took over the land during the 12ᵗʰ Century. Around 1150 a Chapel and cell were erected and were described in ancient texts *'as being in solitude on lands where no man has ever ploughed'* which is an interesting description of a place during times gone by. In 1929 an early Bronze Age burial ground was uncovered giving us an indication of life in this mystifying rough country. Earthworks and a large mound were also found back then, where a large skeleton in a crouching position was uncovered in a grave together with a flint implement. This does seem to be a typical way of burial for the Beaker People from the Neolithic period of our history.

In the more recent era of World War II, Stormy Down

became an RAF station in 1940 and was associated with the RAF Marine Base at Porthcawl harbour. The Free French Air force was also based here. During the war eleven bombs were dropped over the airfield with two unfortunate casualties. The Post Office clerk and one airman sadly died as a result. The airfield disbanded in 1944. This was because the chalk began collapsing due to the rain. The site was then used for various RAF training schools and gliding clubs, but ceased all activities on 28th February 1947. In October 1948 Stormy became a surplus inactive station and some old huts were used by building workers who supplied the Steelworks in Port Talbot. One hanger was moved to Sophia Gardens Pavillion in Cardiff, but collapsed in 1982 due to heavy snow. Other uses for the empty airfield included a motorcycle training centre, cement works and a weekly car boot sale and market. Today it is a solar energy facility and windfarm.

Stormy Down with its fascinating history seems to attract visitors of the supernatural kind, one of which I have seen with my own eyes.

Witnesses have experienced the sight of a black coach pulled by four horses with a lone driver wearing Victorian dress at its helm, travelling at speed past the now abandoned quarry, only to vanish in an instant. What could this re-enactment be for and why would it be travelling on a lonely road in a world he would not recognise today?

A phantom officer in RAF uniform has been seen around the tower on the airfield. But it is only during the month of May. This spectral hazy image seems to display himself as being bewildered and lost. Yet with loud banging sounds, crashing noises and footsteps from this area, maybe this is not the case. But why would an airman from a differing era choose May to haunt this tower and is he trapped in a body that was cut short during the bombing of the airfield unable to rest ?

An unseen entity seems to haunt this area also. He is intent on throwing stones and broken glass at the living, displaying an action by unseen hands. Who could this menacing ghost be and why is he intent on terrifying, or even wounding the living? Perhaps the now empty space of solar energy will bring calmness to a once busy place of activity, encouraging the phantoms to retreat from their enjoyment of terrorising the innocents of today.

Tondu

Tondu, or Black Sward in English, is a village about 3 miles north of Bridgend town and was established as a community during the 18th Century when coal mining began in the area.

But it was during the 19th Century that the village began to thrive when the Ironworks and Iron Smelt Mill were founded by Sir Robert Price in 1838. He purchased Tondu Farm (now Ecodysgu) which had previously been occupied by William Bryant whose establishment went into liquidation. A brick works was also constructed using the clay from the carboniferous coal to make a variety of bricks, mostly for engineering. These were developed alongside the Dyffryn Llynfi and Porthcawl Railway line giving easier access to transport goods. It began trading under the name The Glamorgan Coal and Iron Company. Unfortunately, a trade recession hit communities in the early 1940s. In 1843 black-band ironstone was discovered 6 miles away in Maesteg, which revived the iron trade, prompting Sir Robert to open up Tywith Ore mine at Nantyffylon, which did close for a short while.

The iron trade went into decline in 1850s and Sir Robert faced bankruptcy. But it was fortunate that during his earlier years of trade (between 1843 and 1847) Sir Robert had built up reserves and the potential of such a business was picked up on by John Brogden and Sons from Lancashire and they bought the whole industry in 1854. John Brogden sent his son James who was an enthusiastic 22 year old man to run the business on his behalf. A new lease was signed for 99 years and James set to work on expanding the works and eventually employed a workforce of 900 men. He then rebuilt Tondu House which employed a further 20 men.

The Brogdens had pride in re-opening the coal and copper/ore mines which included 7 other neighbouring villages with the management remaining at Tondu. They also obtained an Act of Parliament to build more railways and merge the 2 railway companies extending as far as Porthcawl. Blast furnaces, coke ovens, kilns and a lift tower were also included in the plan.

After John Brogden's death in 1869, his eldest son Alexander was drafted into the business and he succeeded in opening the Llynfi, Tondu and Ogmore Company, which was a short-lived enterprise and collapsed in 1878, plunging it into administration. It was taken over by North Navigation Collieries Ltd. in 1889.

However, a catastrophic explosion rocked the

community on 26th August 1892, the day of the annual St. Mary Hill fair. This happened at the Parc Slip colliery where 112 men and boys lost their lives. Memorial stones were erected around the area to commemorate the deceased. This tragedy prompted the management to rework the site as an opencast mine. Also in that year, John Boyd Harvey was appointed the Managing Director.

In the 1960s the mine closed and today it is owned by the Wildlife Trust, thus handing over the site to nature with woodlands, wetlands and a meadow.

Tondu House was where the General Managers and their families lived right up until 1940. This was because it was in an isolated position. It was used during the years of World War II, but demolished in 1963. Evidence of its existence can still be seen today.

The magnificent Church of St. John is a modern edifice built in gothic style and towers above the community.

Because of its historic past it would seem inevitable that ghostly activity is rife throughout the area.

The vision of a man wearing a grey overcoat and a flat cap, typical of 1930s dress has been reported to walk an invisible pathway leading to the ironworks. Said to appear during the summer months this spectral image disappears in a hazy mist. Could this man be a past employee roaming around a place that he once called his native land?

The chilling sight of a bright glowing blue ball seems to hover above the Church before descending downwards into the grounds and vanishing into thin air.

Could this unusual entity be an eerie reminder that the people of yesteryear who still linger on a planet unrecognisable to them in today's modern world?

The silhouettes of a man, woman and boy seem to shadow the woodland around the old colliery, only to disappear into oblivion. Could these images be a family from our past unwilling to take their place in another world beyond our grasp?

The tall chimneys of the old earthworks seem to emanate mysterious smoke motions, yet its usage in this way is now buried in our past. But could the labours of yesteryear still be present in its own eerie way?

Vale of Glamorgan County

Barry Island

The famous seaside resort of Barry Island (known in Welsh as Ynys y Barri) gets its name from St. Baruc from the 6th Century. It looks out across the Bristol Channel and remained as an isolated island until the 1880s.

Barry Island was first documented in 1087, when the Vikings invaded the waters around the area. Evidence of Stone Age settlements have also been found by archaeologists, who unearthed Mesolithic flint tools at Friars Point, as well as Bronze Age burial mounds or cairns.

Immigrants are thought to have flocked to the area, where indications of both Bronze Age and Iron Age Celtic cultures inhabited the island. A Celtic British Tribe called Silures also left their mark. Even the Romans are thought to have occupied the islet. It was during the Roman era that St. Baruc, who was a disciple of St. Cadoc, visited the island and on being sent back to Flat Holm to retrieve notes to read to the people from St. Cadoc, his life was taken from him in the form of drowning in the treacherous waters of the Channel. His body was buried in a Chapel which was dedicated to him in Friars Road, where its ruins are still visible.

The island would probably have been overshadowed by woodland during ancient times, so it would only be possible to reach it by boat or on foot across the sands at low tide. But over time, the trees were felled to cultivate the land for farming.

The leisure park was founded by Vernon Studt from

Bavaria, who began his life on the island dealing with horses before opening the first showground on Barry Island beach in the late 1800s.

During the 1880s, Barry Island (or peninsula as it is also known) became connected to the mainland because Barry town began to expand. Barry docks were established by David Davies and opened by the Barry Railway Company in 1896 when the railway line was completed to carry steam trains.

Butlins, the popular entertainment centre was built on the hill at Nell's Point and was the smallest camp built in UK, opening for business in 1966. Over 800 chalets were built to accommodate people seeking holidays for amusement. Butlins sold the business in 1986 to Majestic Holidays. But the camp eventually closed in 1996 with the land cleared by 2005.

Wales is known for its tales of myths and legends and Barry Island seems to hold its own account of folklore and ghostly tales:

The hazy image of a lady dressed in old-fashioned clothing is understood to walk the hills around Whitmore Bay. It is not known who she was, but why would this lady want to revisit a place that would be unrecognisable to her today in a modern world beyond her understanding?

On clear, moonlit nights in the depths of the Bristol Channel, a mysterious ghost ship is said to trawl the seas around the island, only to vanish into thin air. Could this distinct image be a ship from a bygone era, or just an illusion of the mind?

Within the grounds of the Pleasure Park, the ghost train is thought to attract visitors of the supernatural kind. Trucks inside this fearful attraction have been known to run along the tracks on their own accord for no apparent reason. One story expressed an unrecognisable passenger travelling in one of the trucks, only to disappear in an instant. Who could this mysterious person be and could they have had links with funfairs from a departed era, curious with the modern world?

The legend of aliens circling the skies around the island is a modern mythical tale. They are said to descend on the area in search of fish and other modern foodstuffs. But is this a story of fantasy, or just a tale of make-believe?

Boverton

The hamlet of Boverton (or Trebefered in Welsh) lies a short distance east of the parish of Llantwit Major and 4½ miles south of Cowbridge in the Vale of Glamorgan. A hamlet is a settlement that has no Church.

Located on the Boverton Road, this locality is thought to have been founded by William the Conqueror, where he built a castle in 12th Century. However, it was Robert Fitzhamon who took the credit for the stronghold's creation, so its origins remain a mystery.

Boverton actually dates back to the Bronze Age period, with evidence of Iron Age and Roman relics found throughout the area. Boverton derives its name from the Latin for Berton which is the Roman fort of Bovium, as it is understood that the Romans settled here too. It was also the hold of ancient Princes of Morganwg, which was where a baronial fortalice was owned by the Lords of Cardiff before falling into the hands of the Seys family.

During the Middle Ages Roger Seys, who was a landowner and Attorney General of Wales, rebuilt the castle between 1587 and 1589. The daughter of Griffith Vos married Roger Seys, giving indications of how the castle remained within the family for generations until the middle of the 18th Century. It was then abandoned and left to the elements of nature, which inevitably forced it into a ruinous state. Evidence of the castle's remains can still be seen today.

A sizeable manor house is also known to have stood near the site of the castle and was called Boverton Place. It was given to Griffith Vos (Vaulx) by Jasper Tudor (uncle of Henry VIII). King John I was also hidden within the manor house by his estranged wife, which had mysterious factors concerning the signing of the Magna Carta. This tale could be an artifice of folklore, as he did sign this important Charter in 1215.

On its outskirts and within walking distance of the village, Stout Bay, Penry Bay, the pebble beach of Limbert Bay and the Seawatch Centre at Summerhouse Point can be reached. The Seawatch Centre stands on high cliffs about a mile from the village and was originally built in the 18th Century on the remains of an Iron Age fort.

In the 1820s, a new farmhouse was built, appropriately named Boverton Place. It was constructed within the grounds of the ruinous castle and possibly on the site of the old manor house. It was during this century that information about the community of Boverton was written in a column by John Marius Wilson in the Imperial Gazetteer of England and Wales. This took place between 1870 and 1872, so the village gained publicity at that time.

As with many towns and villages throughout the county, it was during the 19th Century that Boverton attracted many differing trades including a now forgotten tannery. It was also the time of the Industrial Revolution and villagers would travel to nearby locations in search of employment.

From 1936-1961 The Welsh Land Settlement Association, established by Captain Crawshay, took over the running of Boverton Place. His enterprise then expanded over time to include a model farm of 650 acres. He employed people from the mining communities who had become unemployed because of ill health or disability, so he was therefore a distinctly caring person.

Today Boverton holds very little trade except for a few shops, a post office and the Boverton Castle public house. But its historical roots still remain as a topic of conversation.

With such a wide variety of historical figures for such a small rural community, it would seem that Boverton is no stranger to occurrences of the supernatural kind.

The phantom image of a lady dressed in black with a scarlet bodice and flouncing blue petticoat parades Pont-yr-ysbryd (haunted bridge). Her tall dark exterior give the impression of holding her arms in akimbo and her life-like appearance seems to be in search of someone or something. But who (or what) could she be looking for and why does she seem so intent in lingering in that particular area? However, quarrymen from our past found the mystifying remains of 2 skeletons abandoned behind a hedgerow, so could this mystic lady be hunting for her earthly corpse hoping for a Christian burial?

Around Boveron Place, the shadowy figure of a lady wearing old fashioned clothing has been seen on many occasions stalking its grounds. Eerily she chants the name 'Wissa' into the atmosphere, sending shivers down the spines of those who hear her. Could this solemn-looking lady be Hadwisa, the divorced wife of King John who was affectionately known as Wissa to locals, or just another case of vicarious imagination?

Castle Upon Alun

This quaint place hidden amongst the winding lanes to the east of St. Brides Major holds a multitude of ancient landmarks.

Originally named Old Castle Upon Alun, it is thought to

date back to the 12th Century with a village and castle. This small area can be located in the hills overlooking the river Alun. After the 15th Century when it was known as Coflein, the whole area was then identified as Castle Upon Alun, Coed Y Wallas or Castle upon Alen.

Castle Upon Alun as we know it today is thought to have contained a castle or strong house, although no sufficient evidence of conflict has been recognized. The castle is thought to have been of Welsh pre-Norman times with many stone arches built in the area. These were probably part of a farm or maybe the castle, although 2 arches have been incorporated in a nearby wall. An archaeological dig unearthed 3 ancient graves from the Roman-Celtic era of the 1st Century with artifacts such as iron spears and daggers found on the site.

Old Castle Down overlooks the village below and Daffodil Wood (Coed-Y-Bwl). This area is also so nicknamed 'BlueBell Wood' because of the carpet of bluebells spanning the area during the springtime. Over a quarter of a million wild daffodils were thought to have been planted during the 19th Century by Mrs. Nicholl. They were locally known as TWM DILIES.

The old footbridge known as Packhorse Bridge is another fascinating characteristic as it is now classed as an ancient monument. This curious landmark, which is also known as clapper bridge, dates back to the 18th Century and tapers from 1m to 1.6m in width with a ramped deck. It was constructed using rubble stone with 5 small gaps of around 1m in length to allow the water to flow freely through it. The footbridge is 28m in length to allow access to the land beyond the Alun River. Clapper bridges are named as such because pack-horses or donkeys would cross upon it and the sound of their hooves on the stone made a clapping noise.

The old brick railway bridge is situated north of Castle Upon Alun and was built by owners of local mines to link collieries between Bridgend and Barry. The station and railway were closed in 1961.

The Ford at Pont-U-Brown which has 16 stepping stones reaching out across it so that during the winter period people are able to reach the other side. They cross the river Alun (Afon Alun) and are known as Stepsau Ddion and are thought to have been a location for film crews from a bygone era. The Ford normally dries up during the summer months allowing access for cars to reach destinations beyond it.

Castle Upon Alun contains other buildings of monumental importance which include Castle Upon Alun House garden and Cartshed, the 17th – 18th Century Ty Maen Barn and other farm buildings.

Most surviving woodland has many a haunted tale to reveal and Daffodil Wood in Castle Upon Alun is no exception. During the hours of darkness, strange blue light anomalies seem to linger amongst the trees, yet no logical explanation has been found. Could these eerie lights come from the people of yesteryear yearning to be remembered from beyond their territory?

The terrifying feeling of being followed by an unearthly person trailing behind the living whilst walking beside the River Alun has been felt, only for victims to realise that no physical person is there. Why would a spiritual entity want to prey on innocent victims from a world beyond their understanding?

The chilling echoes of heavy footsteps, tramping across the footbridge have been heard, only for observers to realise that no physical person is performing this terrifying deed. Could these sounds be from a ghostly being unaware that we now live in the modern world, or just an overactive imagination spearing thoughts into the innocent?

Another legendary tale of the frightful Yr Hen Wrach

(the old hag) is thought to haunt an area close to the ford. Described as being around 6 feet in height, she violently disappears in a flash, emulating the weight of wickedness into the atmosphere.

Colwinston

Colwinston (or Colwinstone as it was sometimes known) is a sleepy village 4 miles west of Cowbridge, or 3.9 miles southeast of Bridgend. Also called Tregolwyn in Welsh, Colwinston lies in the Vale of Glamorgan county.

The 12th Century Norman Church dedicated to St. Michael and All Angels contains memorials to the Thomas and Pritchard families of Norman origin. The Church dates back to 1111 and was restored in 1879 according to a Topographical Dictionary of the Dominion of Wales, written by Nicholas Carlisle who described the village as 'the building ravaged by fire' in 1871. It is situated amongst rolling green fields, enclosed within 14 or 15 acres of land and 60 acres of common pasture. According to a Diocesan report from 1809 the village status of Vicarial Tythes and Augumentation had a Benefice value of £111.18.0. However, Records from 1801 state that 235 residents dwelt within the parish. Around its Churchyard a distinct cross containing a pillar is probably from more ancient times.

By 1835, a Seion Presbyterian Chapel was built and although not much is known about it, the Chapel was converted into a dwelling in 1996.

In 1843, another place of worship named the Ebenezer Baptist Chapel was established and finally completed by 1852. Its last minister was Rev. A. E. Powell of Balarat in 1944.

Colwinston did not escape the perils of conflict as Cromwell's Model Army from the Civil War are said to have plagued an area called The Golden Mile, which is a section of road on the modern A48 road to Cardiff. This is where the Army queued for a mile to receive golden coins, hence its name.

Although this is a logical explanation, the road could have received its name from a different conflict between two neighbours, Iestyn ap Cwrgan, Prince of Glamorgan and Rhys ap Tewdwr. The Golden Mile in this instance comes from the mile of golden coins given to Iestyn by the Norman Baron Fitzhamon in exchange for his daughter's hand in marriage.

Another interpretation of The Golden Mile involves a traveller who was ushering cattle to market in London. He decided to rest at this point in a shady spot and was alarmed to witness an old grey fox creeping towards him.

The fox spoke to the traveller, informing him that he was distressed with sorrow. As the traveller laughed at this apparition, the fox became angry and said that he was Einon ap Collwyn, a traitor to the Welsh Army who fought with Norman Knights. He had been cursed for his defection and would have to spend eternity in the form of a fox. Legend states that the Welsh believe the fox to be the 'devil's spy' who spreads bad luck across the land. Witnesses to the grey fox indicated morality within their family.

Colwinston acquired the name 'the Thankful Village' as it was declared as only one of 52 in the United Kingdom and 3 in Wales. This is because there were no fatalities from both WW1 and WW2.

Agatha Christie was a welcome visitor to Pwllywrach Manor House, situated close to the village. She had become aware of a tale of folklore involving a Gypsy curse on one of the tracks roads. With her fascination for this mysterious tale, she based her book 'The Hollow' on it. Her descendants are said to have remained within the area.

Legend maintains that the ruins of kennels at Pwllywrach emanate eerie screams and cries at midnight on the first Monday in August each year. These pitiful sounds are said to be from a huntsman who went on a drinking binge for many days, leaving his hounds unattended in the kennels and doomed to starve. On his return, the angry hounds tore him to pieces within their confinement. To this day, ghostly mastiffs of hell hounds howl and bay in union with the huntsman's merciful cries around the ruinous kennels.

The mystifying bwgan is said to emulate around Crack Hill in the autumn twilight. He is said to eerily drag innocent hiker's bodies down with a heavy force and therefore reduce them to a slower pace of walking. Described as something or someone pressing heavily upon the back and shoulders, this strange sensation would be accompanied by a mysterious and unearthly shape and described as a man from the Victorian era bellowing out the words 'O Lord, I pray Thee. Deliver me of this burden.' This story of the 'Devil of the Crack' has since been passed down through the generations.

The sight of a quivering horse halted at the top of Crack Hill has been seen accompanied by a frightful bundle rolling down the hill, only to shatter in an explosion of light. Could this frightful image be illusions of imagination, or possibly peculiar tales passed down through the depths of time praying on our minds?

Flat Holm Island

The limestone island of Flat Holm lies in the Bristol Channel, around 4 miles from Lavernock Point in the Vale of Glamorgan. It is classed as the most southerly point of Wales and is steeped with many historical aspects.

The more recognised origins of Flat Holm date back to

the Mesolithic period of around 15,000 years ago. However, during the Ice Age Flat Holm was joined to the Somerset coast as the sea level was much lower in the Severn Estuary before the Ice Age took its grip on Europe. As the ice began to melt, most of the land flooded and therefore creating small islands such as Flat Holm and neighbouring Steep Holm. On its northwest point large fossilized ripples from an ancient era were discovered recently and the site was designated as a Site of Special Interest (SSSI)

Bronze Age settlements from 900 – 700 BC were discovered by archaeologists. It was known as the Ewart Park Phase because a Bronze Age axe head was found in the vicinity as late as 1988. During the 6th Century St. Cadoc (a native of Gwent) visited the island. He lived as a hermit here for 7 years, often praying with St. Gildas, a monk and priest from Scotland who occupied Steep Holm Island.

The Anglo-Saxons and Vikings also stamped their own legacy through documents by Gytha Thorkelsdôttir, the mother of Harold II from the Anglo-Saxon Chronicle of 1067. She stayed on the island before travelling to France. Robert Fitzhamon, who was a cousin to William the Conqueror, formed the Shire of Glamorgan and Flat Holm fell within the boundaries of the 2 parishes of Cardiff, laying claim to the islet.

A farmhouse was constructed on the site and Henry VIII leased the island to Edmund Tournor, whose descendants remained on the island until the late 17th Century who passed the lease to Joseph Robins to farm the land on the west beach.

Other artifacts discovered on Flat Holm came through a survey conducted by Howard Thomas in 1979. He unearthed potsherds from the medieval period, middens (waste heaps), a numerous amount of animal bones and oyster and cockle shells. He also found fragments of pottery from the late 12th 13th and 14th Centuries, as well as sandstone roof tiles and traces of demolished medieval buildings.

Flat Holm originally acquired its name from the Anglo-Saxons who called it Brandanreolice. This originated from the Irish word meaning churchyard, which probably related to burial grounds at the time. However, Holm means island of an estuary in Old Norse, a prevalent indication that the Viking Fleet from Brittany led by Other and Hroald who had taken refuge here after their defeat by the Saxons and Watchets.

In 1815, Thomas Turner visited Flat Holm by boat. He became stranded on the island for a week due to high winds and during his time on the islet stumbled across 2 Christian graves in a field. Eerily one had already been prized open revealing the skeleton of a man. His marble headstone had the engraving of a Celtic cross which had split in half over time. The second grave revealed more macabre skeletons which had been doused in lime. This could have been a practice used when people had contracted contagious diseases and the lime would have been used to sterilize the bodies in the belief that it would eradicate the disease.

The island was also home to miners digging for silver or tin and is more famously known for receiving the first ever radio message across the water by Marconi in 1897. It was also an ideal location in more recent times for the television programme Torchwood to be filmed. In 2011, a public house was opened to welcome visitors to the island with welcome refreshments.

The island is under a 99 year lease and is owned by Cardiff City Council.

The Glamorgan coastline seems to be a graveyard for olden shipwrecks, a subject which has fascinated me since childhood. Many vessels had fallen victim to the treacherous waters of the Bristol Channel, ever changing tides or freak weather storms, plunging them into a grizzly fate.

One particular account involved the passenger ship Tapley which became a casualty around Flat Holm Island in January 1773. It was journeying from Cork in Ireland bound for Bristol and it was caught in a gruesome storm. Seven passengers lost their lives as a result of this tragedy.

Rock islands around Flat Holm are known as 'The Wolves' and they also hold the key to tragedy. On 23rd October 1817 these perilous rocks claimed the lives of 54 passengers from another ship called the William and Mary which was en-route from Bristol to Waterford. After the recovery of 50 of the bodies, they were buried on Flat Holm Island, but the other 4 remained unaccounted for and feared lost at sea.

Flat Holm seemed to be a magnet for lost ships and in 1938 the steamship called Norman Queen ran aground, but was thankfully refloated to continue its journey. But the plight of another steamship called Middlesex was not quite as fortunate and was doomed to be lost.

In 1730s it was declared that lighting was required upon Flat Holm Island to warn ships of its dangers and these came in the form of a brazier which was mounted on a wooden frame high upon the eastern side of the island. But the Society of Merchant Ventures proclaimed that this was a failure and made a petition to erect a more stable structure in the form of a lighthouse. This attempt initially failed as it was declared that no application had been made to the Crown. Unfortunately another disaster occurred which resulted in 60 soldiers perishing in the cruel seas around the island in 1736.

William Crispe of Bristol leased the island for 99 years from John Stuart and was more successful in the quest to construct a lighthouse in 1737. He submitted a proposal to build a solid structure funding all building work himself.

The lighthouse tower finally began operating 1738.

On 27th December 1790 the top of the tower of the lighthouse was severely damaged by lightning, but the keeper managed to scramble to safety. The structure was in desperate need of repair and the oak beams supporting the platform replaced.

In 1819 a more powerful lantern was introduced in the updated tower which was restructured to reach a height of 89 feet and 164 feet above the water.

In 1881 a clockwork apparatus was installed to rotate the light and after buying the lease to the island in 1822 Trinity House installed a fountain oil lamp into the tower and by 1929 accommodation was increased to house keepers. The lighthouse operated smoothly from then on up until 1988 when the lighthouse was automated and its keepers withdrawn. In 1997 solar power was introduced and operated from the Trinity House Operations Control Centre in Essex.

The Grade II listed foghorn building was built in 1906. It contained a siren which gave out 2 loud blasts at 2 minute intervals and could be heard for miles

Flat Holm Island is an ideal location for ghostly beings and a frequent visitor seems to be a gentleman wearing a flat cap and old fashioned clothing. Said to roam the entire island, he makes his presence known to innocent bystanders before vanishing in a hazy mist. Who could this strange phantom be and why does he still remain in a world now beyond his grasp?

Mysterious bright lights have been reported by observers from the mainland. They seem to move in slow and low directions, hovering above the landscape before disappearing as quickly as they appeared. Could these strange anomalies be traditional corpse candles which are eerie illuminations thought to signify death, or maybe an alien force?

The vision of a lady with a pale complexion washing herself in the sea has been witnessed. Alarmingly, she seems to have a black tail splashing behind her, giving indications of a mermaid. But do these creatures really exist, or is this a flight of the imagination?

Although the foghorn has lain redundant for many years, the chilling sound of its eerie blasts are said to have been heard bellowing out across the seas, yet no explanation for this sound can be found. Could the ghosts of yesteryear be guiding vulnerable ships away from the dangers of invisible rocks guarding the island?

During the chilling times of winter, the spectral images of a man and a woman have been seen aimlessly gliding along the coast only to disappear in an instant. But who could these phantoms be and why do they linger on a planet now beyond their recognition?

Strange light anomalies have been seen stretching out across the coastline of the island, yet nobody can explain their significance. Normally occurring on moonlit nights, why would such an extraordinary display frequent an area mostly inhabited by wildlife and birds?

The unnerving sight of a sailor wearing old fashioned clothing is reported to wander the cliffs as if in search of something or even someone. But where could this sailor have come from and why has he not found peace in another world beyond our understanding?

Flemingston

The small village of Flemingston is in the Vale of Glamorgan, around 3 miles south of Cowbridge and 8½ miles north west of Barry. Flemingston overlooks the valley of the River Thaw. Other names that are known in connection with the village include Lanmihangel y Twyn, Treffelemin, Michaelston Le Mont or Flimstone.

At its heart is the Grade II listed Church of St. Michael the Archangel which was built upon 11th Century foundations during 14th Century, although the majority of the Church evolved in 19th Century. This stone structure has a slate roof and contains a monumental stone slab exhibiting the effigy of a 14th Century lady whose name was possibly Elizabeth and thought to have been a member of the Fleming family.

The Fleming family originated with Sir John le Fleming who was granted the Manor Houses of St. George, Flemingston, Wenvoe and Llanmaes. He was one of the 12 knights who came to the area with Robert Fitzhamon during the time of William Rufus. He married Amicia who was the daughter of Baldwin Magnus, Lord of Whitney.

By 1317 Flemingston was held by Philip le Fleming and continued down the line of the family until William Fleming sold the estate to Lewis Thomas of Bettws as he failed to produce a male heir. Further in time the Wyndhams of Dunraven took hold of the estate. Much of the Manor, now a farmhouse, was given a Grade II listing in 2002, including the detached kitchen, garden wall, house ruins as well as its farm buildings. Its 19th Century barn was listed in 2003, as it was detected that it had undergone 16th and 17th Century renovations.

Gregory Farm (Yr Hen Ffern Dy) dates back to 17th Century with extensions and refashioning occurring during both 18th and 19th Centuries. This white rubble farmhouse was awarded Grade II listed status in 2007.

Other buildings and monuments of interest include the rectory in the northern part of the village which is surrounded by a wooded garden and Rose Cottage with its thatched roof and 'eyebrow' windows from 16th/17th Centuries. Another Grade II listed monument is the telephone Call-Box which sits north of the Church.

Flemingston Court Farmhouse dates back to the first half of 16th Century and is Grade II listed. There are a few possibilities what it was used for such as: a rectory, or maybe a steward or farm manager's house. The remains of a castle at Flemingston Court, or Fort Manor, adjoin the Churchyard, which was in Jacobean style and as it bordered the Churchyard, there is a memorial in dedication to Edward Williams (1745-1828) and his son Taliesin. Edward was a famous writer known as Iolo Morganwg, as well as a stone mason and antiquarian who was born in the village. The memorial was erected by Caroline, Countess of Dunraven.

In 1811 Flemingston was described as the 100th of Cowbridge by author Nicholas Carlisle. But by 1870-72 it was declared as being within the boundaries of the county of Bridgend according to John Marius Wilson's *Imperial Gazetteer of England and Wales:* although today it is back to its original county boundary.

Wales seems to be littered with tales of ghosts lurking in the background and it would seem that Flemingston has no immunity: The legend of winged serpents circling the skies around the area is a tale passed down through time. A nineteenth century woman claimed that her grandfather had killed a winged serpent and kept its carcass as evidence. The corpse was then buried with him when he died. But is this a story just a tale of make-believe?

The shadowy phantom of a large dog has been identified prowling the grounds of the Manor, before instantly vanishing like a silhouette in an instant. Could this menacing canine be a guard dog from an era now beyond our perception?

The chilling sound of a phantom bell can be heard, bellowing out across the land from the Churchyard, yet no human action of this kind is said to ever take place. Said to signify a death within the neighbourhood, could this macabre sound be a fable passed down through the depths of time by idle gossips indicating no truth in the tale?

Flemingston's marshy land from the River Thaw, holds a secret tale of a legendary Waterhorse that helped an old man cross the marshland during a horrendous storm. Within hours of this animal appearing, the marsh seems to flood by an imaginary freak tide, frightening people for no valid reason.

But why would a spiritual entity want to prey on innocent victims by portraying fairytale incidents from a world beyond their understanding?

Llanblethian Castle

The sleepy village of Llanblethian lies 1 mile southwest of Cowbridge with attractive houses looking down on the area below. A gentleman called Thomas Carlyle wrote about '*The cheerful group of human homes clustered like a sleeping cataract of white houses with trees overlooking and fringing it dotted over the hillside overlooking the village in a hollow*'. Carlyle's friend John Sterling (1806 – 44) lived at Llanblethian. He was a journalist and critic on the affairs of the Peninsula War, writing about military matters as he was a retired Army Officer. He lived over the brow of the hill at a guest house overlooking the Church and castle.

Once named St Quentins, the listed Llanblethian hillfort (also known as Caer Dynnaf) is set on the hillside. It is thought to have evolved from the Norman period as a ruinous building of rectangular shape with 1.2m thick walls. It has donned the landscape from around the 1200s, which is a typical reminder of Norman construction. However, the surrounding walls and gateway were additions by Gilbert de Clare from 1307, which were sadly not completed until after his death in 1314 at the battle of Brannock.

Other parts of the hill fort include ruinous semi-octagonal towers to the southeast and southwest corners. The ivy-clad gatehouse is bordered by towers and arrow loops (holes). It also had a passageway to a coiled staircase to the rear and the remains of a keep are still visible 10 metres south of the gatehouse. The gatehouse once had guard rooms on each side and was in service as a prison for a long period of time. It was reportedly 3 or 4 storeys high and built over earthworks from 14th Century. The fortress was held by the Lord of Glamorgan and also had connections with the Herbert and Fitzhamon families, who had all disappeared from records by the first quarter of 14th Century.

The castle was used by many Lords of Glamorgan until the late 19th Century, when it was downgraded to a cowshed. With very little remains of such a grand building, it was given to the state in 1994, with the 14th Century gatehouse undergoing restoration by CADW.

Llanblethian Church is dedicated to St. John the Baptist and stands on the hill behind the castle leaning towards Llysworney. Iron Age remains were found here, as well as evidence of Roman existence within the vicinity.

Legendary tales are aplenty around the area of the castle, the most famous being of its people claiming to outsmart the devil. St. Quentin is said to have conducted battles with the evil one around the area. He is supposed to have wounded Satan, leaving him lame for 3 days. Eerily relating to this fable, it is the slopes on the hills that are reported to hold the marks from the battle and have been named 'The Devil's Right Knee Cap and Left Foot', because of the severity of his wounds.

Another mystifying tale involves pixies who are described to be wearing red military uniforms. They seem intent on dancing around the castle site supposedly guarding it from attack. But where could these little people have come from and why would they want to parade around an area outside their normal habitat?

The startling image of a gracious looking lady in red has been seen floating around the top of the gatehouse, only to slowly fade away into nothingness. Could this strange spectacle be searching for someone from another world beyond our understanding, or just an illusory trick of the mind?

Visitors to the castle have reported the feeling of being pushed, only to discover that no physical person is performing this mischievous deed. Could the inhabitants of yesteryear be trying to remind us that this once enchanting building was their home, or just a misjudgment of emotion at such an ancient location?

The distorted cloaked figure of a man has been seen walking around the embattlements as if in human form. What is this creepy image and why would it choose to roam an area unrecognisable to him today as its outward appearance is an antiquated ruin?

An ancient soldier wearing a suit of armour has occasionally been seen around the gatehouse, wandering as if in search of something or someone. But who could this gallantry warrior be, and why would he want to return to a place beyond his spiritual realm?

An implausible story, passed down through the generations of time, conveys the sighting of a headless dog, which is said to have belonged to a giant who roamed the hills. He is alleged to have decapitated his canine companion by accidentally tugging too harshly on the dog's leash. Is this a tale of folklore or a real event which ended in tragedy?

Llandow

The hamlet of Llandow (Llandw/Llan-Dwy in Welsh) lies 4 miles west of Cowbridge through the tranquil lanes of the countryside. Llandow was the proud host of the Eisteddfod on the old airfield between 4th and 11th August 2012.

In the past, a large extent of Llandow fell into the hands of estates owned by distinguished families from the surrounding locality such as Dunraven, Carne and Franklen. Many streams flowed through the vicinity, winding into the River Alun, but most are thought to have become victim to liassic limestone which gobbled up their existence.

The ancient Grade II listed Church of Holy Trinity is held by Llysworney and believed to have its origins from the Normans between 12-13 centuries. Its eye-catching porchway holds the mysterious effigy of a 14th Century lady, although it is unclear who she was when she lived on the earth's plane. The Church is small in size with a parsonage house dating back to similar times of construction. It is enhanced with a saddleback tower, which is thought to have been a lookout against the threat of invasion.

The Church farmhouse, or the Glebe, is also a listed structure with a medieval thatched roof from 16th Century.

Llandow's other medieval asset is the well or Ffynnon and Drindad, the well of the Trinity.

Further interesting buildings that feature in this sleepy village include Ty Teilo, which is a diocesan retreat house, that was at one time a stable block for a Georgian Rectory and now holds a chapel, meeting room and luscious gardens.

The Great House (which has attached flanking ranges) can also be identified as Ty Draw, which is Grade II listed. Built in the 17th Century with Tudor arched doorways, a large fireplace and stone stairs, it was once the central point of the community. Its 3 tier barn was added during 18

Century.

The enigmatic castle ring work lies on slightly elevated ground to the south/southwest of the Church where the knight's fee was held by William of Winchester in 1262. It is classed as being of monumental importance, although there seems to be no evidence of any kind of ancient building work in the area, so mystery surrounds its existence.

Another principal landmark of Llandow lies adjacent to the village in the form of the now abandoned WWII RAF station and airfield which opened in 1940 for service during the war years. The base had a reception, storage and dispatch unit for RAF aircraft as well as other wartime hangars including unit B flight with warplanes such as vampire fighters and spitfires. The airbase was closed in 1957.

An horrific air disaster occurred on 12th March 1950, sending the whole community into mourning. An Avro Tudor V airliner crashed on approach to the runway returning from an international rugby match in Dublin, killing 80 rugby supporters and 5 crew members. Only 3 passengers survived the tragedy.

In the lonely lanes leading to the village, the lifelike figure of a forlorn lady wearing a white robe has been seen wandering through the area as if in search of something mysterious, before vanishing through the hedgerow. Who could this phantom lady be and why does she seem so desperate to locate something from a world now beyond her understanding?

The eerie image of a young girl limping as if injured haunts the lane too. This frightful manifestation then disappears in a flash. Why would a ghostly child want to recreate an action that caused her distress in a life of days gone by?

Precisely on the first Monday in August, the piercing

sound of cries and screams can be heard bellowing out across the land. Could these pitiful noises be from a man who was torn to pieces by hell hounds on this day many years ago in Colwinstone whose cries can be heard many miles away?

The redundant airfield seems to be no stranger to ghostly activity. The haunting vision of vaporous red flashing lights have been seen in the distance, coupled with the silhouette of a Second World War pilot, silently walking across the old airfield only to fade away in a white mist. Why would such a courageous serviceman want to return to an area immersed with sadness from that harrowing time of conflict?

Llanmaes

The village of Llanmaes lies north of Llantwit Major in the Vale of Glamorgan. It sits around 2 miles from the Glamorgan Heritage Coast at Stout Bay.

The Church of St. Cadoc (St. Cattwg's) was first mentioned in documents from 1254 and is believed to have been built upon an earlier Celtic groundwork. It was awarded a Grade II listing in 1963 as it has impressive features such as the chancel, the nave and western tower. Although most of the Church was built earlier, the three bells, the tower and chancel were added in 1632. Other entries referring to the Church date to 17th July 1621 with another quotation stating that the chalice is from 1549.

A wooden rood (screen) divides the chancel and nave and the large font with spectacular rolled mountings on its rim date back to Norman times. A railed tomb devoted to the Nicholl family to the east of the chancel was given Grade II status in 2003.

In the Church dedicated writings are visible worded in Latin which translates as *'This Belfry was erected at the* cost of the parish and friends (well-wishers) to Edward Llewelyn and Iltyd Nicholl, wardens of the Church 1632'. Sir John Nicholl, relation to Iltyd was born at the Great House, north of the Church.

Pre-Reformation murals have more recently been found during renovations of the Church which include one of St. George and the Dragon, which is one of only 3 paintings to have survived within the country. Another mural fresco portrays three priests in Eucharistic robes together with a relic communion plate.

In the Churchyard, a 15th Century Grade II listed Calvary stone cross with four stone steps is a prominent feature.

Burial records refer to the long life of many residents referring as far back as 1495. An unusual allusion suggests that a Battle of Bosworth field veteran Ivan Yorath in 1485 was 108 years old, something which sounds highly unlikely from that era. In fact at the age of 44 he is documented to have lived out the remainder of his life as a fisherman in Llantwit Major.

There is evidence of the remains of a 14th Century Norman Hall or tower called Malifant/Malefant Castle, although no documentation about these erections has ever been unearthed. These sit behind a modern house in fields along the coastal road, where the ruins of a Roman fort are apparent.

Llanmaes House was built around 1540 by James Turbevill. It was Grade II listed in 1962 and is adjacent to the Church situated in the ancient part of the village. Little is known about its inhabitants as documentation does not seem to exist, except that it was enlarged during the 19th Century with a central stairwell and panelled rooms. A drawing room and reception hall were added during 18th Century. The Great House itself is lime washed with a dovecot (Grade II listed 2003) surrounded by beautiful

86

gardens. The three storey building was constructed in renaissance style. The walls, gate piers and gates were awarded Grade II listed status in 2003.

The focal point of this idyllic village is the village green with its vibrantly painted pump and a wooden bridge stretching across the stream which flows through the heart of the village. The Blacksmiths Arms is the only surviving public house in the village, and it gets its name from the old forge which lies opposite.

With such a varied history throughout the years, the tranquil village of Llanmaes may not be as peaceful as it may seem as it attracts visitors of the supernatural kind.

The eerie image of a tall man has been seen on numerous occasions. He has been labelled as the Pedlar's Ghost as it is thought that he was a door to door salesman of Scottish decent murdered in a lane near Picketstone. His large skeleton was found buried beside the roadside, a macabre find for any innocent. Could this ghostly specter be in search of a respectful burial, unable to rest until this endeavour is complete?

Another lane/track road at Llanmaes is eerily called Gallows Way, aptly named after the Gallows Tree where many citizens met their end. The startling spectacle of phantom black dogs have been seen prowling the lane as if in search of someone, or even something. Could these frightful hounds be the faithful companions of the condemned guarding the site where their former masters met their grizzly end?

At the dead of night, peculiar noises have been heard together with the sound of a mass crowd invisibly running along the track road followed by something heavy falling to the ground. Could all of these mysterious occurrences be linked to the treachery of our past, unable to enter their new world unknown to us?

Llanmihangel

The quiet little village of Llanmihangel is a small settlement 2½ miles from Cowbridge and dates back to the medieval period. The village's appearance confuses, as it is a world apart from modern-day living and has been classed as 'taking a step back in time'.

Llanmihangel is first documented in 1166 as a grange area and in the possession of John Norrays. Its stunning Grade II listed Church, which is still lit up at night using oil lamps and candles, was first recorded in 1254 and built with Norman foundations. Dedicated to St. Michael and All Angels, it is furnished with a small font, stone benches in the porch and a harmonium for musical accompaniment.

The Church has a sense of peace and tranquility in its secluded surroundings. An 18th Century silver chalice is set on the south wall and a Holy well which was restored in 1707 by Sir Humphrey Edwin before his death in the same year. Sir Humphrey's monument is set within the church, with his son Samuel (died 1722) and grandson Charles buried beside him

Plas Llanmihangel was a fortified manor house. But evidence of its earlier existence was found in relation to the church which was constructed to serve the owners of the manor during ancient times.

Prior to Sir Humphrey's occupation of the manor, the Thomas family had been living at Plas Llanmihangel during 15th Century. They had links with the Herberts, Earls of Pembroke. Leirez Thomas Ddu of Baglan made considerable changes to the manor in the 16th Century and it was during the outbreak of the Civil War that the estate accumulated extensive debt and the manor was sold to Sir Humphrey Edwin. The house was then extended. Sir Humphrey was an upstanding citizen of the community, a wealthy nouveau-riche merchant and Lord Mayor of London. He was knighted by King James II in 1697 and chosen as the Sherriff of London and Middlesex and Prince of Orange, (1690) before retiring to live within the manor house in this charming village.

The beautiful gardens were his idea and he named them 'The William and Mary Gardens', which included evergreens, orchards and lines of yew trees with a pond. The gardens are Grade II listed in the Register of Landscapes, Parks and Gardens of Special Interest in Wales. The grand garden once had a well and over 100 trimmed yew trees, in line with the fashion of the late 17th Century.

Today, just over 53 inhabitants live in the area and Plas Llanmihangel is now a guest house.

Legendary tales from the turn of 15th Century relate to witchcraft and its 'evil' magic potions'. It is thought that during those dark times of desperation where hope came to folk in the form of such tonics, a local heiress was labelled a witch. Hunted out by locals, they thrust an iron ring around her waist to single her out as 'evil', leading to her suicidal death by drowning in the pool. Her hazy image has been seen rising up from the depths of the water, only to disappear at the blink of an eye. Could this ghostly apparition be the 'Lady of the Ring' the legendary heiress who took her earthly life away from misery?

The mystifying figure of a little green man with piercing green eyes conceals himself amongst the trees, hoping to prey on passersby. What could this frightful image be and where would he have originated from?

The misty vision of another lady with long flowing locks has been identified walking around the woodland, particularly during stormy weather. She seems to dash hurriedly amongst the trees before vanishing. But why would this ghostly person want to seek shelter in a world beyond her realm from a paradise beyond our understanding?

Haunting screams have been heard bellowing out from the hillside at the dead of night, yet no physical person is known to perform these chilling sounds. Could this deafening echo be a chilling reminder of the perils of our past or just tricks of the mind?

Monknash

The small village of Monknash lies in the Vale of Glamorgan. It obtains its name from the monks of Neath Abbey and contained a manor house and large farms within its community during the 12th Century.

The lighthouse buildings of Nash Point beside Monknash date back to 1832 after a passenger steamer named Frolic ran aground on a sandbank out at sea with the loss of 40 lives. With such tragedy, two lighthouse towers were built 1000 feet apart so that ships sailing up the channel had warning of the imminent danger. Floating buoys were also anchored onto the sandbank. Originally painted in black and white stripes, the highest tower stood at 37m high. The lighthouses were the last manned structures in Wales, with the last keeper leaving his post on 5th August 1998 handing his duties over to computerised lighting and fog horns.

Nash Point itself dates back to the Iron Age where the remains of a 700BC fort have been identified. Evidence of the Roman invasion was also found, although most relics have been destroyed by the treacherous waters of the sea and erosion of the cliff face.

Around 300 hooded monks lived at the farms in Monknash and supplied grain and other produce to Neath Abbey.

One legend is about the monks who unlawfully brewed

and drank their own beer, opening a brewery to make money. Unfortunately the Abbot of Neath Abbey became furious by their endeavours and ordered the monks to cease their dishonest trade. The message they sent to the Abbot read '*No beer* – *No grain*' as they had no intention of bringing an end to their operation. The Abbot was forced to let them continue otherwise he and the monks at Neath Abbey would go hungry.

A lady wearing a lurid outfit has been seen by visitors outside the lighthouse apparently playing a cello, yet no sound of music is heard. She looks aimlessly towards the raging sea as if waiting for someone before disappearing in an instant. Who could this lady be and why would she want to remain around such an obscure environment?

The alarming sound of an old fashioned fog bell has been heard at the dead of night bellowing out across the sea. Could this ghostly sound be warning modern vessels that danger lurks beneath the perilous tides?

The hazy image of an old fashioned mariner has been spotted, appearing to eerily float around the lighthouse. Could this unusually dressed gentleman be that of a sailor from a vulnerable ship lost in the depths of the raging seas?

The vision of a young boy has been identified wandering around the cliff's edge only to disappear in a split second. His Victorian-style clothing seems dirty and torn as if his life was evilly snatched from beneath him. Could this tragic child be belonging to a past keeper falling victim to the dangerous waters below, or just an illusion?

A story of a clash between two lighthouse keepers who became entangled in a feud concerning the two lighthouses has also been told over the years. Could this legendary tale be linked to the isolation and loneliness felt by keepers and their families during the darker days of our past?

Old Beaupre Castle

This Grade I listed structure was built in the early 14th Century as a medieval fortified manor house. Located in the community of Llanfair outside the town of Cowbridge, it is locally known as 'Booper' or 'Old Beaupre Manor'. It was built in two stages, the first being in 1300 in an L shape which was a fashionable design at that time. The second stage of development happened in 1600 where impressive new features were added. These include the three-storey gatehouse and a carved porch decorated with columns inspired by the architecture of ancient Greece and bearing the family's heraldic crest carved in stone.

Other the names for the manor include Beawpire, Bewerpere, Bewpyr and Bewpur.

It is unknown why Beaupre was labelled a castle as it was not actually used by the military for defence, but as a family home for William Bassett, his heiress wife and their son Richard.

During 16th Century (Tudor times) Sir Richard Mansell began the undertaking of the building's remodelling as the original structure was not sufficient for the needs of the modern way of living back then. In 1586 an outer gatehouse was added and the whole building itself was extended to create a middle courtyard, together with a parapet walk overlooking the surrounding landscape. The walk had wonderful views of the riverside and orchards and must have been picturesque.

The Bassett family lived within the manor for generations, until their fortunes declined after the English Civil War.

A legendary tale proclaims that the Bard Meurig Daffydd presented a praise poem to William Bassett, Lord of Beaupre and he read his prose to the Lord. Bassett presented a coin to the Bard as a reward. But after his departure, the poem was thrown onto the roaring fire in the hearth.

The Bassett families became unpopular from then onwards within the community and were frowned upon by their neighbours, as they had become callous with disputes and violent in behaviour. These awkward clashes often ended in court cases.

Old Beaupre manor house was then purchased by the Jones family who decided not to live in the large abode. Instead, they dwelt in a nearby smaller farmhouse. They changed the mansion's name to New Beaupre.

In a sorry state of repair, Beaupre was sold in 1709, as only part of the building was habitable. Windows had been blocked up because of the new levy known as the Window Tax, which was based on the number of windows within a house during 18/19th Centuries. Bricking up the excess windows was intended to avoid this expensive duty.

Today, the roofless ruin of Beaupre is under the care of CADW, although some parts are still in use today.

As with many old buildings throughout the principality, which seem to infiltrate ghostly activity, it seems that Old Beaupre is no immunity.

A fierce-looking phantom accompanied by a black dog is reported to stalk the grounds of this eerie building. He is said to be pointing towards the river in a forceful manner. Could this frightful spirit be trapped in a world he no longer recognises, or is he trying to give us indications of a tragedy that happened many years ago?

Another apparition has been seen around the area in the form of a banshee-like ghost. She has been seen on many occasions and given the name of Gwrach y Rhibin (Hag of the mists) by the locals. Witnesses have reported that she rises from the depths of the river flapping her hands like a bat during the hours of darkness.

Could this heartbreaking enactment be a lost damsel in distress who tragically drown in the river during her time on earth, or just a lost soul yearning to be remembered beyond her watery grave?

The mournful sounds of wailing and sobbing emulating from the ruins of this once magnificent building have been heard on numerous occasions, when no physical body can be seen. Who could be making these pitiful sounds and why would they want to unnerve the gullible?

Penarth

Penarth is seaside town in the Vale of Glamorgan and like many other towns and villages has a multitude of ghostly tales attached to it. I have chosen to write about Penarth Pier as I feel that it has a fascinating but tragic historic past, as well as reported ghostly guests treading its boards.

The construction of Penarth Pier began in 1894. Spanning 219 yards in length it was opened to the public in 1895. In 1907 a wooden pavilion was built to accommodate a dance hall and by 1929 the entrance foyer was added.

A devastating fire in August 1931 ensured the wooden structure's demise as well as the majority of the platform. The rebuilding of the pier took place a short time later, but it wasn't until after World War II that the structure's reconstruction programme was commissioned. In May 1998 the fully restored pier that we see today was reopened for public use.

Glow-Worms were very common beacons before the 1950s and workers from different villages within the Vale would describe the grassland as luminated, particularly at night. People riding bicycles would place these on their hats to see in the dark as lighting was not as common as it is today. Unfortunately, they are no more as times have moved on with more congestion and housing, with less grassland for these creatures to flourish.

The eerie figure of a lady dressed in Victorian clothing has been seen mysteriously walking the full length of the pier, only to vanish at the blink of an eye. Who could this elegant lady be and why would she want to repeat steps in an environment that she would no longer recognise?

The image of a gentleman sporting a flat cap and glasses has been placed seemingly limping towards the far end of the pier before disappearing into thin air. Could this unusually dressed gentleman be a handyman from the buildings past returning to a place that he became accustomed to during his time on the earth?

The shadowy phantom of a large dog has been identified prowling along the planks of the pier, before instantly vanishing like a silhouette in an instant. Could this menacing canine be a guard dog from an era that we would not recognise?

Porthkerry

The old village of Porthkerry is situated on the western side of Barry in the Vale of Glamorgan, and dates back to medieval times where Celtic tribes dwelt within the area. These people were often terrorised by the pillaging Vikings who would scan and raid the coastline.

Cwmcidi was originally a medieval village in existence before the 13th Century. It spanned 280 acres of land, which contained a Parish Church. In 1622 Cwmcidi was known to contain 5 houses and a small dwelling site. But these had virtually disappeared by the 1840s when the Romilly family (landowners of the community since 1412) cleared the area to create Porthkerry Park which has been used by humans for centuries.

They constructed a farm and cottages which housed

employees such as foresters, stable hands, workers at the sawmill and meat butchers by bleeding the woods and fields dry.

The sawmill at Cwmcidi was built around 1835 by the Romilly Family Estate Business with its first employee, Joseph Williams (a carpenter by trade) working the mill and its waterwheel until his death in 1880. Another gentleman named Joseph Williams then took over the business and created a blacksmith and wheelwright shop. He was succeeded by his son George who was the last person to man the mill until the 1920s. The mill ceased trade from that point and it is reported that the abandoned building was used as a local scout headquarters before being left to the elements. It was saved from demolition in 1990.

In 1588, a gentleman called Owen Williams purchased land below Barry Hill, where he constructed a dwelling. One notable abode was named Cliffwood Cottage, which was built in 1583, housing its most famous occupant Ann Jenkin, who was eventually convicted of practicing witchcraft.

Another landmark which towers above the landscape of Porthkerry is the spectacular viaduct. Situated in the Park, it has areas of woodland and greenery on each side and was opened as a railway link to Barry on 1st December 1897. But disaster had already occurred in 1896 when one the 13 archways slipped, resulting in the line being closed on an immediate basis. During the time of its closure, this stone structure was found to have unstable foundations and other faults, so during its time of repair, a loop line was created about 2½ miles in a northerly direction.

On 8th January 1900, the railway line opened to carry goods trains and on the 9th steam trains were permitted to carry passengers.

The Park today is known for its golden stairs, which acquired its name from the rumoured golden coins buried beneath it during construction. This and Cliffwood (a lowland wood on limestone rock) were designated an SSSI (Site of Special Scientific Interest) in 1962 and 1983.

The fable of a man and his servant travelling to visit a local witch to purchase a love potion has been deliberated for centuries. As they refused to hand over payment for the remedy, a curse was thrust upon them and they were never seen again. In their place 2 mysterious trees appeared, one tall and straight, the other shaped in a crooked way. Could Ann Jenkin from Cliffwood Cottage be the witch in question, who cast her spell over the men eager to test her magical remedy, or just a myth passed down through time surrounded by mystery?

A tale of mystery involves the woodland where large black hounds with red piercing eyes accompanied by riders on horseback have been seen prowling the area at the dead of night, only to disappear in a shocking way. Why would fearsome creatures from a distant era want to roam this vicinity intent on terrifying people from the present?

Legend maintains that winged serpents with jewel-laden wings hover around the area of the Park and if witnessed, are considered to bring good fortune to bystanders in the form of money or valuables.

With such an intriguing history and ghostly phenomena it seems that Porthkerry does live up to its reputation of affection from days gone by.

Stalling Down

Stalling Down is an open hilly area of land a few miles east of Cowbridge. It also has connections with St. Hilary in the Vale of Glamorgan and was once known as Stallington.

Stallington is most famous for its crusade which is reputed to have taken place in 1403 between followers of

King Henry IV and the Welsh leader Owain Glyndŵr as part of the Glyndŵr Rising of 1400-1415, also known as the Welsh Revolt.

Its leaders Rhys Gethin Cadwgan (Lord of Rhondda) and Owen Glyndŵr, initiated the battle against the English army, which took place on a site locally known as Bryn Owain meaning Owain's Hill. The crusade is thought to have lasted for around 18 hours with a heavy defeat for the English, who retreated through Cardiff pursued by the Welsh. The weather was appalling with fiery thunderstorms which brought about a violent flow of flooding.

The Welsh forces from Morgannwg, led by Rhys Gethin (Swarthy Rhys) included a French lobby group to enhance their soldiers, adding more strength to the Welsh crusade. Battleaxes were thought to have been the weapon of choice and were named *the bloody axe* because of the bloodshed throughout the conflict.

In 1896 archaeologists discovered that an oak plank in the floor of Llanblethian Church (3 miles away) was hiding a stone stairwell leading down to a crypt where the gruesome discovery of 300 male skeletons lay strewn, as if *buried* in a hurry. This ancient crypt stood 7ft in diameter together with an archway and vaulted roof. It was covered by earthworks to conceal it from the outside world. People from the deeply religious Victorian era were horrified and gave each a Christian burial in consecrated ground within the newly renovated Church and Churchyard to help them rest in eternal peace. A pew inside the Church contains a small inscription as their burial place in dedication.

A monolith on Stalling Down was erected in memory of the soldiers of Glamorgan Yeomasonry, together with suggestions that an old road, ancient cross and hillfort once stood there at the time of the conflict, although no obvious remains of such relics are apparent to us today and may have been lost through the test of time.

Historians from 1995, however, question that the battle ever took place as the records from the time of the conflict have no mention of it, spreading doubt throughout the locality. Its earliest reference was found in ancient manuscripts by Iolo Morgannwg from 18th century who declared that Stalling Down never existed. His revelation was followed up by other writers including Edwardian author Arthur Bradley who compiled a biography of Owain Glyndŵr in 1901; although he declared that the battle did take place in 1405. He called it *'The Battle of Bryn Owen'*. The uncertainty of Morgannwg's account upset the traditions following the battle, straying people's minds into believing it was a manifestation of the mind. This sent citizens into frenzy for hundreds of years until it was confirmed that the battle had indeed taken place on Stalling Down. If the earlier writings were correct and no battle took place, why were the bodies of 300 soldiers found at Llanblethian Church?

The people of today also believe Stalling Down was a place of public hanging between 16th and 17th Centuries.

Stalling Down has an air of mystery and eeriness surrounding it, which includes the unnatural sounds of ghostly moans coupled with disembodied arms emerging from the ground. These images are often orchestrated by the beating of drums bellowing out across the land.

Could these startling reverberations be from dying soldiers yearning for help after the fierceness of the crusade?

People have also reported the chilling sound of men fighting an invisible battle, coupled with the thundering of horses' hooves charging across the slopes of the down, yet no physical exploit is ever seen by the living. Why would another enactment take place on the loneliness of the down?

A phantom black hound which is thought to have some sort of association with the site has also been witnessed. It is accompanied by the clanking of chains dragging, an eerie encounter for any innocent. Its presence is short-lived as this unsettling spectacle disappears in a spooky mist. Why would a hound cloaked in chains want to re-enact such a deed, and what would be its connection with Stalling Down?

A phantom knight on horseback appears on the anniversary of the battle, a date that remains unknown to us. He seems to be followed by other apparitions charging as if in defence. The ground is also said to bleed after a storm which could relate to the end of the conflict where Henry IV's army fled. But could these images be real, or just a mass figment of imagination signifying a conflict which may have taken place so long ago?

St. Brides Major

The village of St. Brides Major lies in the Vale of Glamorgan. It is named after St. Bridget of Ireland and probably dates back to the 12th Century when the Parish Church was constructed in Norman style by Simon de Londres. This ancient treasure became a listed building in 2002.

The splendour of the Parish Church towered over the village and was a congregational centre for people throughout the community during ancient times. Inside the building are monuments of dedication to upstanding citizens of the district who were considered important, one being Arnold Butler and his family. Two monumental plaques are also on display in the Vestry from the Bryn Sion Calvinistic Methodist Chapel which was erected in 1859 and classified as a listed building in 2001. By 1987 the Chapel was no longer in use and became the site of residential housing.

St. Brides Major as a community relied upon its many wells and springs for water and although some were covered up, others can still be seen. Pilcot Pool was named Avon Dawel or Silent River, as it ran underground after a few yards and could no longer be heard. The landscape was dominated by agriculture where farmers would employ local people to farm the land, needing water from the wells to tend to livestock.

In the vicinity near Blackhall, evidence of lime kilns were found. These were created to burn timber so that walls could be built to keep sheep in enclosed areas, giving indications of habitation from our past.

Jacob's well can be found near a turn in the road feeding from the Alun river.

Pant Marie Flanders well is situated near Heol-y-Mynydd and has been declared an ancient monument.

St. Brides Major was littered with stone quarries during the olden days and also had individual trades such as village stores, blacksmith's shops, a police station, a village hall, a bake house and various cobblers.

Other interesting structures from our past include the medieval Preaching Cross within the grounds of St. Bridget's Churchyard, the school bell tower, the War Memorial dedicated to the bravery of local servicemen and women located in Bull Hill and Pont Groes Gwta which is a listed bridge built in the 18th Century.

Penance building ruins can be found in the area which are thought to have been a secluded home for the Monks of Margam Abbey, who had struck up acquaintances with local women and were exiled here to ask forgiveness for their sins.

One forgotten public house in the centre of St. Brides Major was The Greyhound Inn, which is now a dwelling. It was a popular 'watering hole' for many groomsmen whose employers visited the local church and the groomsmen moored the horses outside the Greyhound Inn and with free time on their hands, would quench their thirst with local ale.

The lifelike image of an elderly lady wearing old-fashioned black clothing with a flowing skirt has been witnessed wandering up an imaginary road only to disappear as quickly as she is witnessed. Who could this lady be and why would she want to walk through a village that she would probably no longer recognise?

On the pathway leading to the village shop, the shimmering effigy of a donkey kicking out at an invisible building has been seen, only for it to fade away into the background. Could this frightful image be a replay from the time when blacksmiths from the village would tend to the needs of shoeing animals, or just tricks of the minds of its witnesses?

My parents lived in St. Brides Major during 1960s and my mother witnessed the phantom sound of galloping horses upon the common whilst walking her 2 poodle dogs during the hours of darkness. As the stampede got closer to her, she could see that they were headless, with no course of direction. Could this terrifying commotion be from another world beyond, or gruesome ghostly displays from an unknown ancient battle?

Swanbridge and Sully

The hamlet of Swanbridge lies on the coast overlooking the Bristol Channel, 4 miles south of Penarth. The island of Sully across the bay is an islet which can be cut off by the tide that frequently blankets the causeway, therefore forcing it into isolation.

It is unclear where the name Swanbridge originates from; but it was at one time a working harbour as documents from the 16th Century specify that skippers of boats were obliged to pay a levy to local officials for transporting their wares from distant shores into the port.

In 1569 two thousand blocks of cheese and 80 barrels of butter were impounded by an official as the captain of the vessel from Penarth had not paid his duty tax. The harbour (or Creek as it is sometimes known) also acquired unwelcome immigrants from shores beyond the Channel. Goods, both for import and export, were transported to neighbouring towns and villages via St. Mary's Well Road. Iron mooring rings can still be seen on the eastern side of the bay, as a reminder of the trades of days gone by.

Swanbridge became linked to other destinations around the area by the Taff Vale Railway line, where its people could travel in style to other destinations around the country. Swanbridge Halt was built in 1890, but became another victim of the Beeching axe in 1968 and was left abandoned, or bought by businesses who sold its rail tracks for scrap.

Archaeologists unearthed evidence of Roman and Viking visitation and a Bronze Age fort with a stronghold barrow in the area. A Danish Iron Age Buttress which occupied the eastern side of the island, together with the Bronze Age Barrow and post medieval port on the northeastern side were all then listed as monumental landmarks.

Across the foreshore of Swanbridge lies the island of Sully, which is only accessible via the causeway and can be cut off by the rapid incoming tide.

Thought to mean 'South Lea or Pasture', it gets its name from the Norman Knight Reginald de Sully from Devon who built a small fortress on the island for protection against pirates.

Today, the remains of a small wall are the only evidence

of its existence.

Sully Island had become a haunt for pirates, with 'Alfredo De Marisco', the Norman pirate known as 'The Night Hawk' who based himself here in the 13th Century. This was the beginning of the notorious smuggling trade. By 1330, Lords of Avan (d'Avene) had purchased the Island and in 1348 Hugh le Despenser, Lord of Glamorgan, acquired the land. Later the islet was sold to Sir Thomas Stradling, an upstanding citizen throughout the whole community of Glamorgan at the time.

Sully's most famous ship wreck was the SY (Survey Yacht) Scotia. This ship originated as a sealer vessel named Hekla from Norway. Its captain was Tam Robertson and during the Great War the vessel became a freighter, which unfortunately caught fire around Sully Island. Its diminished keel then sank into the depths of the hungry sea.

Sully Church is dedicated to St. John the Baptist and stands on an ancient edifice containing a silver chalice dating from 1567. The Church became a listed building on 22nd January 2000.

The Captain's Wife is a public house at Swanbridge, haunted by the wife of a ship's captain. It once spanned 3 cottages to house fishermen, sailors and their families. Appropriately, it was named Sully House as it overlooks the harbour and Sully Island. This 'watering hole' and restaurant opened its doors for trade in 1977.

Legend maintains that Captain Winstanley was commanded to sail on a voyage to Jamaica by his lover's disapproving father. His daughter was then forced to marry Colonel Rhys, a man with an upstanding position. The marriage was not a success because his wife pined for her lover. So when Captain Winstanley returned from his expedition, secret meetings were arranged for the lovers, only for them to be discovered. Colonel Rhys was killed in a duel between the rival men and the lovers then eloped together at sea, but were burnt alive in a fire within their cabin. She is said to haunt the house that she shared with her husband, in search of her true love.

Another twist on this legendary tale involves a captain taking his wife on a voyage at sea where she dies of a fever en route. Not to arouse suspicion, he places his wife's corpse in a lead-line box. On return to Swanbridge, he buried her remains in the woods. The coffin was subsequently stolen, denying her a Christian burial. Her soul of unrest haunts the area and her hazy image is reported to stalk the woodland wearing a black dress.

Another account of this sinister tale claims that the captain rowed his deceased wife ashore at the dead of night and hid her body within the house, where it was stolen. When the building was renovated, the eerie discovery of a skeleton was unearthed in the woods behind the abode. Could this fearful find be the remains of the Captain's Wife?

Tinkinswood

Tinkinswood is close to St. Nicholas in the Vale of Glamorgan and was once an ancient village some 6000

years ago. All that remains now of a probable bustling settlement is its burial chamber. Siambar Gladdu Tinkinswood (its Welsh equivalent) is also known as Castell Carreg Llech-y-Filiast. It is a megalithic structure made during the Neolithic period in our history. It is a customary edifice typical of structures built in Europe and is called a dolman, which has an outward appearance of a large capstone and smaller stones (made of limestone) supporting it. The top stone weighs a staggering 40 tons and is 24 x 14 feet long. Its construction would have employed around 200 strong and sturdy men to lift it into position above the smaller stones and was probably then covered with a mound of soil. It is a long wedge-shaped cairn containing a rectangular stone chamber and decorated by a horned forecourt with dry stone masonry and a herringbone pattern.

The presence of the stone-lined pit remains a mystery, but it is believed that the bodies of the dead were left exposed to the elements for a short time before being interred into the chamber for a cultured burial. Typical of the period, soft red Neolithic ware and Beaker style pottery were buried alongside their loved ones in the hope of eternal life. These burial traditions probably carried forward into the Bronze Age era.

Thought to be the largest burial chamber in Europe, Tinkinswood is situated on a sloping valley which would have had a desirable outcome on village life at the time. The valley came equip with a stream for necessary water, good soil for growing crops and suitable stone for constructing tombs to give the deceased an honourable place of rest.

The site of this amazing burial chamber was excavated in 1914 when the remains of 920 human bones were discovered, which lay scattered in broken pieces. The archaeologists established that at least 50 people were buried within the chamber from the 'New Stoneage' period in our history. Within the hollow Neolithic and Bell-Beaker style pottery was unearthed, giving indications that it was in use over a long period of time. Ceremonial pots were buried with loved ones in memory of them, and this type of pottery was also unearthed during the excavation. The Neolithic people were thought to have been ruthless and would deliberately break or give away their most treasured possessions, for what reason remains unknown. But this theory would explain the fragments of pottery found in 1914. Following the excavation, parts of the site were reconstructed. A pillar was inserted for support and its outer walls re-clad.

The site is now managed by Cadw and the structure is rated as a monumental building within the heritage of Wales.

The Neolithic people were probably the first individuals to discover the skill of farming. They also began to produce their own pottery for cooking, storage earthenware and burial pots.

There are many legends, or even myths, rebounding from such chambers of an ancient era, which include spending time after nightfall at the sinister tomb. Performing such a vigil would result in that person either going raving mad, becoming a victim of instant death, or emerging as a poet. The mound or mountain top and its surrounding stones were believed to be women who had been cast into stone for dancing on the Sabbath day, a macabre belief shrouded in mystery. Could this legend be the reason for a person's downfall way back in time?

Another legend of folklore associated with dolmens was the Merry Maidens which were also known as Dawn's Men. This was not linked to the sunrise at dawn; but is a version of Dans Maen which means Stone Dance in Cornish. It is a similar legend to that of the Merry Maidens as 19 women were cast into stone for dancing on a Sunday. But this tale had pipers playing tunes for the women to dance to. The two pipers were allegedly cast into stone too, only they stand in a field in the meadow to the north east of the burial tomb. These legends may have been initiated by the early Christian Church whose intention was to forbid Pagan rituals being performed.

Legend maintains that burial tombs of this type are cloaked with secrecy, magic and myth and an intriguing tale involves the shoeing of horses around the area of the mound. These good-natured animals would be left alone for a short period of time, in order for their master to prepare for the task. On his return, the horse is said to have been mysteriously shod and the silver coins of payment gone. Was this tale of folklore linked to fairy magic?

Burial chambers have also been known to have adopted the name snivelling corner as the tears of the mourners are said to echo through the chamber and its stones are believed to be weeping. But could these tales be true, or merely a mass figment of imagination from ancient times?

Other Eerie Tales

New Year

The observation of New Year on January 1ˢᵗ dates back to 153 BC, during the rule of the Romans. Before this celebrated date was set, the 25ᵗʰ March was measured to be the beginning of the New Year. But it was not until 1752 that Great Britain adopted 1st January for New Year's Day because it was calculated as the first month on the Gregorian calendar, named after Pope Gregory. The date of this month was considered to be lucky because the full moon on that night would bring hope for the year ahead.

There are many ancient customs surrounding New Year which were believed to bring good luck. One entailed 'burning the bush' which was thought to banish the evils of the past to make way for a new beginning.

On New Year's Day children from our early world would dance from house to house singing songs before noon hence collecting gifts such as coins, apples and sweets. If they failed to complete the singing before midday, they would be labelled as fools.

The 'first footing' tradition at the stroke of midnight gave the belief that the first person to enter through the door would bring good luck for the year ahead.

In Wales, Dydd Calan was celebrated from dawn to dusk. Young boys would carry a cup or jug of water with twigs from evergreen trees and visit houses around their neighbourhood whilst singing. Mischievously they would splash the house dwellers with the water using the twigs in order to receive money. Could this be a tradition of good luck for the year ahead?

Traditions like these are no longer in practice in our modern world, as more up to date methods have replaced them.

New Year nowadays is celebrated with parties, dancing, fireworks and singing the traditional Auld Lang Syne, which originates from the Scottish Hogmanay. At the stroke of midnight, with the last chime from the clock ringing in our ears, it has become customary to open the door to let the old year out and welcome the new one in. This is now our symbol for good luck for the year ahead.

Ghostly tales are still rife around the turn of the New Year and Moor lane in Porthcawl is no exception. This creepy lane is known for its eerie stories and has its own tales of ghosts who enjoy making their presence known around the time of Christmas and New Year. The mysterious sound of church bells has been heard ringing out into the darkness at midnight from an invisible place of worship, sending shivers down the spines of its witnesses. One legend maintains that the bells from a forgotten church are rung out by legendary religious inhabitants from a bygone era. But who could these people be and why would they want to perform this deed in a practice that has no relevance to the traditions of today?

The 19th Century Bridge in Moor lane is known for its supernatural occurrences and at midnight a headless horseman has been seen thundering across it before disappearing at the blink of an eye. Could this chilling image be a re-enactment of an unforeseen tragedy from the structure's distant past or just another misjudged figment of imagination?

January

The month of January (Ianuarius in Latin, Ionawr in

Welsh) is named after the god Janus who was from Roman mythology and means door, as the month is the doorway to the New Year. Its birthstone is the garnet and its flowers Dianthus caryophyllus or galanthus.

The Anglo-Saxons called this winter month wulf-monath, meaning wolf month, or wintarmanoth (winter/cold month).

The 2nd January, through an Old Saxon belief, was one of the unluckiest days of the year; although no real proof stating why seems to have survived. If a baby was born on this day, death was said to be unpleasant.

The 6th January marks the end of the Christmas festival. It is appropriately named Twelfth Night because it brings a close to the 12 days of the festive period. It is the date of the Epiphany on the Christian calendar, a night when the Three Wise Men (or Kings) visited baby Jesus in Bethlehem.

Not to be confused with Shakespeare's comedy play of the same name, (a piece that I studied for both O level and London Academy of Music and Dramatic Art) Twelfth Night has been celebrated over the course of time with many different traditions. But in most cultures it was a joyous occasion overflowing with food, drink and merrymaking.

Superstition stated that all yuletide trees and colourful decorations must be dismantled and put away before the 6th January, as it was deemed to be unlucky. Failure to obey the custom would bring misfortune and disaster into the lives of the defiant.

The 13th is the feast day of St. Hilary who was a Catholic Bishop, born on this date in 368 AD. It is said to be the coldest day of the year as wintry events of frost, ice and snow from our past have been recorded to begin on this day.

The earliest recognition of such events on 13th January date back to 1205 when the River Thames froze over and ale and wine turned to solid ice due to the sub-zero temperatures.

An extract from Stowe's Chronicle states '*So began a frost which continues til 2nd and 12th day of March, so that the ground could not be tilled.*'

In the month of January, between 1550 and 1750, Frost Fairs were held. The occasion had tents, sideshows, food stalls and ice bowling. These festivals took place upon frozen rivers, lakes and ponds and lasted for the duration of 4 days.

The 20th January is superficially St. Agnes's Eve when unmarried maidens and girls would perform rituals before going to bed. They would wish for dreams about future husbands by reciting The Lord's Prayer, fasting all day and finally retiring to bed by walking up the staircase backwards. A 1820 poem by John Keats is a tribute to St. Agnes: '*Ah, bitter chill it was! The owl, for all his feathers, was a-cold; The hare limp'd trembling through the frozen grass, and silent was the flock in woolly fold: Numb were the Beadsman's fingers, while he told, His rosary and while his frosted breath, Like pious incense from a censer old, Seem'd taking flight for heaven, without a death, Past the sweet Virgin's picture, while his prayer he saith.*'

This usually coincided with the first New Moon of the year. An unwashed silk handkerchief was held up and used to stare at the moon. It was believed that the number of moons that could be seen through the handkerchief revealed the number of years until the maiden would be married. On viewing the moon in this way, a chant was recited: '*All hail to thee moon, all hail to thee. I prythee, good moon, reveal to me this night who my husband shall be.*'

Historical events which happened throughout January include:

On 2nd 1770 an enormous Christmas pie was baked. It consisted of 2 bushels (measures) of flour, 20lbs butter, 4 geese, 2 turkeys, 2 rabbits, 2 woodocks, 6 snipes, 4 partridges, 2 neat's tongues, 2 curlews, 2 blackbirds and 6 pigeons. Weighing 12 stone it would be large enough to feed the people for weeks!

On 17th January 1912, Robert Scott and his party reached the South Pole and on the 29th in 1856 The Victoria Cross originated. The medals were actually made from the metals of guns captured during the Crimean War.

With its unusual traditions and superstitions coming to light from ancient times, it seems that January had a devastating effect upon folk from all walks of life.

Twelfth Night

The 6th January marks the end of the Christmas festival. It is appropriately named Twelfth Night because it brings a close to the 12 days of Christmas.

The superstition of dismantling all Yuletide decorations before Twelfth Night relates to Tree Spirits which were thought to live within the greenery of the Yule tree, holly and ivy. All plant-life would have to be returned to its rightful place after the midwinter festival as people believed that spring would not return if the custom was not followed. Natives also deemed the tree to be mischievous unless they returned it to its natural habitat, giving us an indication that the tree, holly and ivy were planted during olden times.

Nineteenth century principles lured people to keep the holly, ivy, yew and mistletoe within the household until 2nd February, which is Candlemass Day, the date that the infant Jesus was presented to the Temple. This day was known as the Feast of Lights because all greenery would be burnt on large bonfires to banish all evil.

During Tudor times Twelfth Night commemorated the end of the winter festival which had commenced on All Hallows Eve, (Halloween) the 31st October. Even after such a lengthy time of merriment, Twelfth Night would be celebrated with the Lord of Misrule and other higher figures of society who traditionally exchanged places with the peasants of the land for the evening.

Large cakes containing 1 bean and 1 pea would be baked and whoever was lucky enough to have these pulses in their slice of cake would crowned King or Queen of the Feast. Also, the taking down of all decorations of holly, ivy, wreaths, fruits and nuts resulted in them being consumed by the King or Queen of the feast: but only until midnight as Christmas would then be officially over and everyone would return to normality.

A popular beverage to drink on this occasion was alcoholic punch called wassail. This was consumed along with Twelfth Night cake. The custom dates back to pre-Christian times when the Celtic festival of Samhain and ancient Roman fiesta of Saturnalia were also observed.

The feast of the Epiphany was also known as Three Kings Day, the adoration of the magi or the Manifestation of God. The Three Kings travelled to worship the 'King of the Jews' by following a bright star to Bethlehem. They were from ancient Persia and were thought to be Median Zoroastrian priests who were sent to present gifts to the baby Jesus of gold, frankincense and myrrh.

Today, the superstition of dismantling all decorations from the Christmas tree still remains, although many people are unsure of its origins. After clearing away the tinsel, it is then time to celebrate with food, drink and parties as Christmas is over for another year. Porthcawl has been the centre of Twelfth Night festivities for many years with the bearing of fancy dress costumes and traditional dancing being the main themes. In fact, my parents and their friends would attend parties each year (when my brother and I were small) at the now forgotten Manor Suite (at the entrance of the fairground) or the Stoneleigh Club which was situated in John Street and sadly burnt down in the 1980s.

Legendary tales state that the ghosts of the deceased would emerge from beyond the grave on this night, transforming themselves into lifelike apparitions. Séances would be performed to entice these spirits to contact the living. This form of communication is known as necromancy.

Magical rituals were also performed to entice the souls of the dead to visit earth once again.

Sometimes the 5th of January is observed as Twelfth Night when the phantom image of a lady riding a grey horse has been witnessed. She seems to ride the plains of the countryside, only to disappear in a hazy mist. Could this unknown apparition be seen throughout the landscape of Wales?

Phantom armies are also reported to parade the roads of Wales as if in search of something or even someone, yet no sound is ever heard.

Spectral ships sail the seas on this entertaining night and the frightful sound of ghostly trains chuff to a halt at invisible destinations. But can these eerie apparitions be tricks of the mind?

February

February is the second month of the year on both the Julian and Gregorian calendars. It acquired its name from the Latin word februa which means purification, superficially making it a Roman month. Along with January, February was not on the original datebook but was added to the calendar by Numa Pompilius around 713BC.

In Welsh, the month of February is known as Y Mis Bach which means little month as it is the only one to have 28 days. Chewfor is the equivalent in Welsh for this dreary time of year as it is the shortest month except for leap year which extends it to 29 days every 4 years.

Around 400 years ago, February was called Feverell and 100 years later it changed to Februeer. February as we spell it today only came into existence around 100 years ago.

Sol-monarth was an Old English term for February which means mud month, as the weather is gloomy at this time of year. It is meteorologically the third and final month of the winter season.

Sol-monarth (cake month) was an ancient event where cakes were offered to the gods. It was also known as sprout and kale monarth as planted cabbage and kale would begin to sprout.

The birthstone of February is the amethyst and its flowers the violet and common primrose. The zodiac signs Aquarius (until 18th) and Pisces are also associated with this month.

The Christian festival of Candlemas (festival of lights) is celebrated on 2nd day of the month. This was because during ancient times the Christmas festival lasted for 40 days until the second day in February. It was a day when all candles to be used in Churches for the year ahead would be lit and blessed in the belief that the flames would protect its people against plague, illness and famine. In ancient times it was known as the Feast of Lights in celebration of the increasing strength of the sun as winter gives way to spring.

Superstitious rituals were performed from 12-14 as it was believed that these dates were borrowed from January. If they were stormy days, the weather for the year ahead would be good: whereas if fine weather prevailed the climate would be unpleasant.

The renowned snowdrop begins to appear around landscapes in February. This beautiful white flower is believed to have evolved when Adam and Eve were expelled from The Garden of Eden. This was because an angel appeared to give Eve hope and guidance. In the hope of banishing cold winters, the angel transformed snowflakes into flowers proving that winter does eventually end and that spring is around the corner. This can be seen in the old rhyme *'The snowdrop, in purest white array. First rears its head on Candlemas day'*

On 8th February 1855 the people of our country were petrified one morning to discover peculiar footprints in the snow in the shape of a cloven hoof. Could this have been a sign that the devil had visited earth and could cast his spell of evil amongst humankind?

The most famous date in February is 14th, the feast of St. Valentine, which is celebrated in many countries around the world. There are a few variations as to who St. Valentine actually was; but the most likely was in honour of the individual who took it upon himself to challenge a Roman Emperor who banned soldiers from marrying during 3rd Century. He became a campaigner for the soldiers, but was executed for his outspokenness in 469AD. Pope Gelasius declared this date in honour of St. Valentine.

Another legend states that St. Valentine was executed for his beliefs in Christianity and before he died he penned a note to his lover saying *'From Your Valentine'*.

The day became associated with romance sometime in the Middle Ages. But I believe Shakespeare's quote from his tragic play Romeo and Juliet seems to celebrate love in an adoring fashion: *'Love is a smoke raised with the fume of sighs; Being purged, a fire sparkling in lovers' eyes; Being vex'd a sea nourish'd with lovers' tears: What is it else? a madness most discreet, A choking gall and a preserving sweet.'*

The Romans and Celts observed February as the start of the spring season.

Shrove Tuesday is a tradition hailing the day before Lent, with the fasting custom marking 40 days before Easter. Also known as Mischief Day, it was a time when Church bells would ring out, a game of football was played by all and feasting and revelry were celebrated.

Ash Wednesday was named after the ash tree when school children would carry a piece of twig in their pocket for luck. Failure to carry out this tradition would result in their feet being trodden on.

The Friday following Ash Wednesday was once called Kissing Friday. It was a day when schoolboys were allowed to kiss girls without fear of punishment. This custom lasted until 1940s, when the War years wilted it away.

Springtime

Spring is one of the pleasurable seasons of the year, as it breaks the transition between the winter and summer. It lasts for 3 months from March to May and is an indication that nature is preparing for new beginnings, when animals and insects re-emerge from hibernation and birds raise their young. Plants, flowers and trees begin their rebirth too.

Spring is a varied season, as throughout the world it is dependent on local climate and time zones.

The spring equinox on 21st March has been declared as the first day of this welcome season and the noticeable increase in more hours of daylight and a rise in temperature are all significant because of the earth's tilt of 23.5 on its axis towards the sun as well as more prominent tidal currents.

In more recent times earlier appearances of spring have occurred with rising temperatures during the winter months sending nature into confusion.

Also known as the vernal equinox which falls between 19th and 21st March, the spring equinox (which means equal night in Latin), was originally introduced by the Romans, who used the lunar calendar to predict the spring season, as they realised that both day and night were 12 hours long.

But it was Julius Caesar who reformed the festival to the solar calendar, declaring the date of the equinox to be 25th March with 365 days in the year ahead and a day extra every 4 years. In 1582 Pope Gregory XIII changed the date back to 21st March because March and April were known for their connections with religious festivals. The main celebration during springtime is Easter, which is thought to derive from Pagan, Hebrew and Christian traditions.

Eggs portray signs of new life and they became traditionally eaten at Easter, taken from the German word Eostre. Eggs were forbidden to be consumed during the 40 days of Lent, where fasting and omitting dairy products from the diet was essential.

It was customary to present friends with red coloured eggs whilst chanting Easter greetings. Red symbolised the blood shed by Jesus during his crucifixion.

Ancient traditions surrounding the spring equinox and Easter include Morris dancing, performed on Easter Sunday to banish the evil spirits of winter.

Another favourite custom was performed on Easter Monday and Tuesday. Named 'lifting and heaving', it required young men to visit houses in their neighbourhood carrying a chair decorated with flowers. They would encourage girls or ladies to sit upon the chair and the men would lift the female 3 times into the air as a sign of good luck for the year ahead. The following day, the opposite was performed where the ladies would tend to the duties of the chair lifting.

The fable of freshly baked bread, made on Good Friday and handed to sailors on ships about to set off on the high seas, was believed to bring good luck for the voyage ahead.

The eerie occurrence of dancing white waves appearing in the vicinity Nash Point around Easter time have been seen. Witnesses have described them as 'Merry dances' when deceased sailors seemed to ride on the crest of the wave as if on horseback. But could these ghostly images be an indication that the departed are still lurking on the seas where they met their end, or just a trick of the imagination

An intriguing legend of folklore involves spring-heeled Jack. Thought to have lived during the Victorian era, he would perform giant leaps into the air at night. He was believed to be tall and thin wearing a black cloak. He had clawed hands with his eyes resembling red balls of fire, breathing out blue and white flames before disappearing into the night.

The ghost of the Easter Bunny is full of intrigue as it is said to only appear once a year on Easter Sunday. Catching a glimpse of this special ghost is said to bring good luck for the year ahead.

Woodland areas are particularly haunted around the time of Easter where wild hunts were traditional. Black hounds are said to prowl the dense forest accompanied by fearsome riders on the backs of horses and goats. But why would these alarming images want to lurk around areas likely to be unrecognisable to them in today's society?

The coastline around Britain also has its ghostly tales where mermaids are said to ring bells hidden beneath the waters of our shores. Witnesses to this spectacle are thought to gain a long-lasting and fruitful life. But could these tales be a matter of folklore passed down through the generations of time?

March

March was originally the first month of the calendar year prior to the introduction of the New Style Gregorian calendar in 1752 from the Julian. It was named after Mars, the Roman god of war, which is from the Roman word Martius.

Meteorologically, the first day in March is the beginning of the spring season: whereas the March equinox on 20/21 marks the astronomical birth of spring.

The birth flowers of March are the daffodil, jonquil and narcissus, which is a wild daffodil. They all symbolise rebirth, happiness and friendship. Narcissus (also known as the lily crocus) comes from Greek mythology and was named after a boy of the same name who was cruelly transformed into a flower. The daffodil and leek are symbols of Wales. It is thought that they were both placed on caps to distinguish between friend and foe during battles, and Welsh people wear them with pride on St. David's Day.

The gemstone for this spring month is aquamarine, which comes from the Latin word aqua meaning water. This gemstone was believed to protect sailors and sea voyages. Its tranquil colour is said to encompass the body with calm and levelheadedness. March's second birthstone is the bloodstone, a darkish green jasper with red spots of iron oxide. The star signs of March are Pisces (until 22nd) and Aries.

A familiar poem to many is by Williams Wordsworth entitled **Daffodils**; a poem that my mother taught me as a child as she adored this particular spring flower: *I*

WANDER'D lonely as a cloud That floats on high o'er vales and hills, When all at once I saw a crowd, A host, of golden daffodils; Beside the lake, beneath the trees, Fluttering and dancing in the breeze.

March, as with other months of the year, holds and array of festival days, which begin with our Patron Saint David on 1st. The Welsh celebrate his life with singing, concerts, parades, the wearing of leeks or daffodils and dressing in traditional Welsh costumes. The daffodil became a popular Welsh symbol in 19th Century when David Lloyd George displayed it at the 1911 Investiture and official publications. But its traditions date back to earlier times.

The 15th March relates to the *'Ides of March'* from the Roman calendar, a date when the month was divided into two equal parts. It was also the date on which Julius Caesar died in 44BC.

St. Patrick's Day is celebrated on 17th March in Ireland. He is their Patron Saint.

The 25th March is known as Lady Day, which is the feast of the Annunciation. But superstition states that if Easter was to fall upon this date disaster would follow soon.

A date that is more recently added as a special day is Purple Day, which aims to raise awareness and funds for epilepsy and is observed on 26th March.

Mothering Sunday falls in March too, which is the fourth Sunday of Lent and has traditions dating back to the 16th Century. It was a special day when mothers throughout the land would be presented with spring flowers at Church services by their children to thank them for all of the care and love they have given them throughout the past year. Today we celebrate it in similar style.

During bygone times, Oranges and Lemons Day was a celebration on 31st, when children would recite the nursery rhyme in Churches, sometimes ringing hand bells as entertainment. They would then be presented with an orange and a lemon after the Church service around a table in the yard.

March is known as the windy month with a traditional proverb from Weatherlore: **March Winds, April Showers, Bring forth May flowers**. Another saying which does not fill us with hope for the months ahead states: *As it rains in March, so it rains in June.*

The final three days in March were said to have been borrowed from April, an old custom relating to the lending of sheep.

Traditional games played for hundreds of years throughout Lent include marbles and skipping. Marbles traditionally came in the form of hazelnuts, cherry stones, pebbles, round balls of baked clay or eggs which were rolled until the stroke of midnight on Good Friday.

Wales is shrouded with tales of folklore, mystery and tales of ghosts and the month of March maintains this tradition:

At the dead of night on 1st March (St. David's Day) the eerie sound of phantom singing can be heard bellowing out from churches across the land. People who hear this are said to be surrounded by luck for the year ahead.

The first full moon of spring seems to attract serene images of a ghostly army marching aimlessly along country roads. Carrying glowing torches of fire, their silhouettes disappear into oblivion.

After the ferociousness of winter, on misty mornings in March, the hazy image of a stricken ship can be seen around the coast of Porthcawl. Said to resemble a galleon, this creepy ship only appears every ten years. Perhaps this disturbing image is making the living aware of its fate on the anniversary of its sinking, possibly in March.

April

April is the fourth month on the Gregorian calendar, but was the second on the Julian datebook.

It is unknown where the name of this spring month originated, but it may have come from the Latin word aperire, which means open, as the buds and other flowers grow again after the gloomy season of winter.

The Anglo-Saxons named April Eostre monarth/Eastermonarth as the festival of Easter usually falls within this month.

April 1st (as we all know) is April fool's day, a time which is known for its fun and practical jokes, which have been practiced for hundreds of years in our country. It began here in 1582 when Pope Gregory introduced the Gregorian calendar and the new dates were moved forward by 13 days.

April fool's day became popular in 1700s when people would do abnormal things compared to other days of the year.

'April 1st, some do say, is set apart from All Fools day.'

But why they call it so is a mystery. Silly antics included looking for a hen's tooth, striping paint, giving left-handed gifts like screwdrivers to right-handed friends and playing numerous other pranks. However, it was declared that such actions should only be performed until midday, otherwise the prankster would be ridiculed with the rhyme:

'April Fool's Day is past and gone, you're the fool and I am none'.

The first Sunday in April was celebrated as Daffodil Sunday, a time when Victorians would pick these cheerful flowers from their gardens and present them to sick people at local hospitals to give them good cheer.

In the middle ages, April 6th was called Candle Day. Candles were placed in Churches with a pin stuck in the bottom and auctions would be administered with the wealthy bidding for a parcel of Church land to let to the poor for a year.

The person bidding at the time when the candle burned down and the pin fell to the floor won the land, a strange custom now buried in history.

The Victorians honoured Primrose Day on April 19th, as it is claimed to be Queen Elizabeth II's favourite flower.

Palm Sunday is the final Sunday before Easter. In 1570, it was traditional for ladies to make pax cakes for parishioners of local Churches.

Ladies of manor houses in the area served 5 shillings worth of cake and ninepenn'orth of ale to all within their Church as a goodwill gesture for the year ahead.

Welsh speakers call Palm Sunday Sul y Blodau, which is a lullaby based on a poem by Eifion Wyn who was born in Porthmadoc (1867-1926).

The custom relating to this day was to decorate the graves of loved ones with ornate flowers and deck them with garlands of rosemary, rue, crocuses, daffodils and primroses in preparation for Easter Sunday, which is the festival of the Resurrection of Christ.

The fable of freshly baked bread, made on Good Friday and handed to sailors on ships about to set off on the high seas was believed to bring good luck for the voyage ahead.

Welsh people had endearing customs relating to Good Friday too. Public holidays were declared on this day as no activities such as work were embarked upon.

Folk would walk to Church barefoot so as not to disturb the peace of the day and long reeds were woven into the shape of a human figure and waved through the air on the journey to Church.

Ancient traditions surrounding Easter include Morris dancing, performed on Easter Sunday to banish the evil spirits of winter.

May

The colourful month of May is named after the Greek goddess of fertility Maia and its traditions date back to the Pagan rituals relating to the last month of the spring season.

May has two bank holidays, the first being May Day celebrated on the first Monday (Belatine) and Whitsun and Whit Monday follow at the end of the month.

Whitsun was symbolised by the dove during the Middle Ages where these birds of peace were taken to Churches throughout the land to be blessed. People from this era often carved out wooden doves or even created birds using the art of paper folding, or origami.

Rose petals would also be collected for the occasion to shower the clergy during the reading of the story of Pentecost. The ancient flower of columbine (which is Latin for dove) is also a symbol of the month of May.

Whitsun is believed to date back to the 12 century, where carvings of The Green Man would mysteriously appear within Churches throughout the British Isles, as green was said to be the colour of life. The Green Man was also believed to be the God of Woodlands, so he was obviously an ancient 'God' portraying the beliefs of its time.

Also on Whit Sunday, keepers of lighthouses would illuminate their buildings recognizing the symbol of fire, another custom of its time.

Welsh folklore tales maintain that fairies dance around the fairy ring at dusk on Whit Sunday and any witnesses to this silent action are believed to obtain good luck for the year ahead. This tale is another slant from legends of Mabinogion, which means tales of youth in the Welsh language and have been passed down through time.

Wheels of fire were rolled down the hillside and livestock would be guided through the flames as a sign of purification, a custom which is now thankfully resigned to the history books. Another belief involved Druids worshipping trees as a religious ritual.

If hares are found close to your home, they are deemed as witches in disguise and luck would never cross your path for the year ahead, especially if they were killed. This belief was another custom concerning the month of May.

History also has interesting facts concerning events surrounding the month of May from a bygone era. For instance, on 8th May 1945 V E Day (Victory in Europe) was celebrated, the Roman god Mercury (son of Zeus) marked his birthday on 6th and the more macabre events included the burning at the stake of Joan of Arc on 30th in 1431 and the death of King Arthur in 542 on the same date.

The ghostly figure of a lady dressed in a long flowing gown and presenting herself with long scraggly hair has often been associated with the month of May. She is chased by riders on white horses thundering through villages to capture her. But who could this maiden be and why would she have to flee from a supposed cavalry?

A re-enactment of a mediaeval (or possibly Roman) feast occurs late at night on the evening of the third Tuesday in May where a phantom scene of unrecognisable people seem to sing, dance and huddle around a small bonfire on hillsides around the countryside, yet these actions are said to be performed in silence. Could the people of yesteryear be unwilling to abandon their celebrations from the Christian calendar, sending reminding thoughts to the living?

Phantom officers wearing military uniform have been reported to patrol the area of their old base at St. Athan at dusk throughout the month of May, yet no explanation can be found for their appearance. Could the participants of WWII be reminding us of their bravery during such a fierce battle, or just phantoms revisiting a barracks which celebrated the end of the War?

May Day

May is named after Maia, the Greek Goddess and the ancient tradition of May Day dates back to Pagan rituals during the season of spring. The celebration included young men and women dancing on the village green where a decorated felled tree (usually birch) would be the centre of the festival. Branches were cut off the tree and the trunk decorated with coloured ribbons tied from the top.

May Day was originally a communist proposal celebrated around Europe on International Worker's Day, but it was not acknowledged as a bank holiday until the British Labour Party introduced it in 1978.

May Day was called Beltane, which was an ancient Celtic festivity where bonfires were lit to mark the beginning of summer.

During the middle ages, villagers would awake at dawn on the first day in May to collect blossoming flowers and branches to decorate a maypole. A piper would then play tunes for them to dance around it, wearing colourful clothing and belts. Today the costume is more elaborate with white clothing and a red sash.

An additional tradition was to crown the fairest maiden as 'Queen of the May', who sat on a flower-decked chair and was lifted into the air with a doll beside her to represent spring and rebirth. Her suitor would be chosen on 2nd May as the May King. The two led the festivities and were often nicknamed 'Robin Hood and Maid Marian'.

During the Victorian era May Day was known as 'rustic delight' and more customs were included into the celebrations. Houses would be decorated with flowers and greenery in the belief that vegetation spirits would bring good fortune. May wine was also drunk on this day.

Another superstition saw girls washing their faces in the early morning dew in the belief that it would make them beautiful.

The legend of playing tricks on villagers became a tradition for the first day of May during Victorian times too. Beating the bounds involved landowners walking around the boundaries of their property to confirm their rights. It became a day for repairing fences and boundary walls to keep the people at bay for the year ahead.

Superstitious tales maintain that your life is doomed if you go on the water on the 1st day of May.

If hares are found close to your home, they are deemed as witches in disguise and luck would never cross your path for the year ahead, especially if they were killed.

Ghostly figures of a lady dressed in a long flowing gown and smarting long scraggly hair has often been associated with May Day. She is chased by riders on white horses thundering through villages to capture her. But who could this maiden be and why would she have to flee from a supposed cavalry?

Welsh folklore tales maintain that fairies dance around the fairy ring at dusk on May's Eve and any witnesses to this silent action are believed to obtain good luck for the year ahead. This tale is another slant from legends of Mabinogion, which means 'tales of youth' in the Welsh language and have been passed down through time.

June

The month of June comes from the Latin *Junius mensis* which means the month of Juno. It is the first month of the summer season and is a time for celebration as the weather supposedly becomes warmer.

June has a few historic events which changed the way of the world, such as in 1284, the Pied Piper lured 130 children in Hamelin away, in 1799 astronomer William Lassell discovered the moons of Uranus and Neptune and in 1812 German astronomer Johann G Galle discovered the planet Neptune.

But June is probably best known for the Midsummer festival of Summer Solstice which is full of intrigue from ancient rituals, traditions and legends which certainly have mystery surrounding them.

Originally a Pagan and Christian festival celebrated between 20th and 24th June, it was the 21st June that was calculated to be the longest day and shortest night of the year. Solstice means 'sun stands still' in Latin since the sun appears to be idle in the sky, with the whole occasion described as the 'Festival of Madness and Love' because of the power of nature's cycle of the sun and universe.

The celebration of Midsummer's Eve (the Eve of John the Baptist's birthday) is an ancient event where summer plants were picked at dawn because they contained healing powers and bonfires were lit to ward off evil spirits. Also called Litha and the Feast of St. Peter, it marks where the sun tilts on its axis to its maximum strength.

During Neolithic times the lunar calendar was followed and the beginning of daytime with the sun rising at dawn began as a celebration.

During 7th Century, St. Eligius forbade Christians and Pagan religions to perform Summer Solstice rites, dancing, leaping or chanting as he deemed all merriment of this kind to be evil. However, the celebrations then changed to mark St. John's day and the merriment was banished.

The 13th Century monk of Winchcombe spoke of boy revellers who would collect bones and other rubbish to burn on bonfires to drive away dragons, which were thought to poison springs and wells.

During 15th Century people celebrated Midsummer by visiting places of worship equip with candles to pray all night long. But this changed dramatically when feasting, singing, dancing and pure lechery took over, thus turning Holy devotion into sin. Around 1498 the performing of plays with costume clothing and colourful parades had become popular customs until they too were banned in 1675.

Today, the prehistoric monument of Stonehenge is the most popular location most associated with witnessing Summer Solstice where people gather to observe dawn arriving. The volcanic bluestones are thought to have originated from Wales, 160 miles away from the ancient landmark. It is not known how they were transported such a long distance by hand, but the eeriness of their existence is still captivating and full of intrigue.

In Wales, Summer Solstice is called Gwyl Ifan or Gwyl Ifan Ganol Haf, which is the feast of St. John the Evangelist. The occasion included agricultural fairs, dancing and banqueting. Bonfires were also lit to ward off evil spirits with folk dances performed around them. These celebratory rituals died out during the 19th Century.

Legendary practices were performed during ancient times where fires lit on the hillside were very popular and creatures of the land were blessed with fire. They were not used as sacrifices, but were guided through the fire in a sun-wise direction as gestures of good luck.

The date was also marked as the veil between the earth

and the world beyond at its thinnest and that powerful entities would enter our atmosphere. Vigils would be held on the night of 20th June as a focus on driving away these demons. The sacred site of the vigil was believed to give positive powers to all who think pure thoughts. Those who failed in this quest became utterly mad, dead or spirited away be the fairies.

Wheels of fire were rolled down the hillside to represent the sun's power and witches were believed to meet with phantoms at dawn on 21st June to cast their evil magic across the land.

Another practice involved placing fresh flowers under pillows to signify important and pleasant dreams, particularly of love. Flowers and herbs were also hung on doors and windows and placed with the ashes from the simmering bonfires onto the hearth for protection against evil.

With witches dispatching their spells of evil and fairies kidnapping the weak, could Summer Solstice hide a multitude of customs now buried in our past?

At midnight on Midsummer's Eve, the strange sight of a shapely stone seems to dive into the sea and go for a swim, particularly around the coastline of Porthcawl. Could this be the same stone that is said to go for a drink around the time of New Year, or just a fable of folklore talked about by our ancestors?

Bridges throughout the land are no stranger to the fairy population who come out in force on the eve of Summer Solstice. If they are not acknowledged by anyone crossing a bridge, the fairy folk have no hesitation in making their presence felt. But could these be tales of fantasy, passed down through the depths of time?

July

The month of July, (Quintilis as it was once known meaning 5th in Latin) is named after Julius Caesar. It was originally the 5th month of the Roman 10 month calendar, which began in March around 700 BC. Later in time, Januarius and Februarius were added, moving the first month of the year to January.

Tradition at the time stated that odd numbers were lucky, adding July as one of the seven months to contain 31 days. This was in honour of the Roman General Julius Caesar, whose birthday was on the 12th July. The changing of the name from Quintilis to Julius happened in 44 AD.

Reputed to be the warmest month of the year in the northern hemisphere, the Gregorian calendar was adopted, shortening the name of the month Julius to July.

The birthstone of July is the ruby and its honourable flower the larkspur, adding to the fascination of such a colourful month.

July has a few memorable occasions which changed the way of the world, such as the birth of Julius Caesar on 12th, Amelia Earhart and her plane were lost in Pacific Ocean in 1937 and on 19th Apollo 11 orbited the moon in 1969, the day before Neil Armstrong made history by becoming the first man to set foot on the moon.

July is probably best known for the ancient tradition of St. Swithen's Day which is said to occur on 15th. If showers take place on this day, it will rain for 40 days and 40 nights. This tale dates back to 971 AD when the bones of St. Swithen (who died 100 years before) were moved to a shrine at Winchester Cathedral. A horrific storm brewed up on that particular day and it rained continuously for 40 days. People believed that the spirit of St. Swithen was in tears because his bones had been moved from his original place of rest. *'St. Swithen's Day if thou be fair, for forty days 'twill rain nae mair'*, doggerel poetry from the 12th century.

Another Saints day which falls within the month of July is for St. James, patron Saint of Pilgrims on 25th July. This day was also known as Grotto Day, a particular occasion when children would make grottos in caves and decorate them with scallop or seashells as an emblem to their saint. They would then chant *'Please remember the grotto, it's only once a year. Father's gone to sea, mother's gone to bring him home, please remember me.'*

A further Saint to be honoured on 25th July is St. Christopher, the patron of travellers. He was as a martyr killed in the reign of the 3rd century Roman Emperor Decius" or "Dacian who reigned 249–251 AD.

Saint Margaret was a popular saint too and was celebrated on 20th July. She was born in Gloucester and had adopted the name St. Peg and people all over the country would celebrate this Victorian era lady by making a plum pudding called Heg Peg Dump. Honouring her would bring protection against illness and evil spirits.

Customs relating to devil dancing were traditional during olden times, but these were banned during Elizabethan times.

Crop circles (circular patches upon the hillside) appear on flattened fields of standing corn during July. At one time these were believed to be circles carved out by aliens landing upon our planet.

With devil dancing proclaimed to be evil and traditions encoding the weak, could the month of July hide a multitude of ghostly beings waiting to pounce during the seventh month of the year?

Olden roads give the impression of a silhouette of a man who appears to be crawling along invisible surfaces.

Alarmingly, he seems to have no face. Are our highways safe from this spectral image, which seems to be intent on attracting the attention of the living?

Coastlines along south east Wales seem to attract the haunting sight of two small pirate ships in battle. This enactment seems to occur in foggy weather, tearing along our coast before vanishing into thin air.

The eerie vision of blood red rain is said to fall from the skies on the eve of 17th July, an alarming spectacle for any witnesses. The blood is alleged to be from a giant who was murdered by an assassin from a forgotten era. But could this be a tale of fantasy, or just a natural occurrence embroidered on through the test of time.

Tall phantom figures with fire-filled eyes seem to roam hillsides at the dead of night in the middle of the month, their shadowy images piercing the minds of the living. But what could these eerie images be and why would they seem intent on scaring the people of today?

August

August is the 8th month on the Gregorian calendar. Before this Sextilis was the 6th month of the Roman datebook. But 8 years prior to the birth of Christ, the month adopted the name Augustus, which was named after the Emperor Augustus Caesar.

The Anglo Saxons called August Woed which means weed. This was because all plant life grows at a more rapid pace at this time of the year.

The birthstone of August is the peridot and its honourable flower the gladiolas, adding to the fascination of such a colourful month.

August has a few memorable occasions which changed the way of the world, such as the celebration of the National

Eisteddfod in Wales, which dates back to 1176 and usually takes place during the first week of the month. This tradition was originally a medieval gathering of bards and minstrels who competed for the Noble's Chair with a festival of Welsh art and culture.

The Battle of Bosworth began on 22nd in 1483, World War I began of 4th August 1914, Francis Chichester left Plymouth on Gypsy Moth VI on 27th in 1966 and our Queen of Hearts, Princess Diana was killed in a car crash on 31st.

The 1st day of August was traditionally known as Lammas Day, the thanksgiving for the harvest crops where loaves of bread were baked by farmers from the wheat of the first crop and laid on Church altars for Holy Communion. Lammas Day was celebrated with a festival where farmers would also present their workforce with a pair of gloves. One white glove would be placed on a decorated pole to mark the beginning of the celebration, which lasted for 11 days. It was the festival of love and the foretelling of marriage and luck would befall upon any couple whose love blossomed throughout the duration of the fair.

Farmers would also let the bread from the first corn go stale so that they could sprinkle its crumbs into each corner of their barn as a symbol of good luck.

This custom ended abruptly under Henry VIIIs reign as he broke away from the Catholic Church. Lammas Day was renamed Holy Christian Day and the Harvest Festival was forwarded to the following month of September.

The Celtic Harvest Season was called Lughnasadh after the Celtic sun god Lugh and corn dollies were made to mark the occasion.

The hottest days of the year are said to happen throughout August according to Weatherlore and an old saying was repeated during festivals: '**Dry August and warmth doth harvest no harm. The first week of**

136

August be warm, the winter will be white and long.'

The Summer Bank Holiday was introduced under the Bank Holidays Act in 1871. The intention was to give bank employees time off work to attend cricket matches on 1st day of the month. One hundred years later in 1971, it was moved to the last Monday in August.

Customs relating to devil dancing were traditional during olden times, but these were banned by Puritans following the Civil War.

In the Middle Ages, rushes were used as floor covering and villages throughout the land would hold a special summer ceremony on the nearest Saturday to the 5th. Rushes were harvested for the ritual and carpets and sculptures (called bearings) were carried by a procession to people's houses.

Coracle races were held around riverbanks during the middle stages of the month. These mostly involved fishing skills with the catching of salmon and trout, which are noted to be moving upstream from the sea.

With so many legends and eerie tales alike encompassing the southern counties of Wales, could the month of August hide a multitude of ghostly beings waiting to pounce during the eighth month of the year?

On the 1st Monday of August, around the ruins of kennels at Pwllywrach in Colwinston, eerie screams and cries at midnight can be heard bellowing out across the land each year. These pitiful sounds are said to be from a huntsman who went on a drinking binge for many days, leaving his hounds unattended in the kennels and doomed to starve. On his return, the angry hounds tore him to pieces within their confinement. To this day, ghostly mastiffs of hell hounds howl and bay in union with the huntsman's merciful cries around the ruinous kennels.

Zig Zag lane in Porthcawl is no stranger to the haunting sight of a coach and horses tearing along at pace. Legend maintains that the coach driver and his female passenger tragically died after he lost control of his coach, overturning in the darkness of this staggered track. The phantom figure of a lady dressed in white clothing appears to wave at witnesses from a carriage before the whole scene disappears into oblivion. Could this be a re-enactment of the tragic incident from days gone by, or just an elusive trick of the imagination?

Autumn

The colourful season of autumn is from the old Latin word autumnus and autompne in the French language. Traditionally this event occurs between 21st and 24th September each year.

Fall often refers to autumn and the term fall is the Old Norse word for feallen and the old English for fwell.

The first day of the 'fall' takes place with the Autumnal Equinox which is said to begin around the 22nd September. The word 'equinox' comes from the Latin for equal night and is one of the only days of the year that the sun crosses the celestial equator, which is spherical in shape, similar to the Earth's equator.

The days begin to get shorter and nights longer from the time of the Summer Solstice (21st June), but with temperatures dropping during the months of September, October and November, it seems to be that our world is in preparation for the winter months. The leaves transform in colour and begin to fall from the trees, with wildlife changing its normal routine to suit the occasion by hoarding food in readiness for hibernation or migration to warmer climes.

Britain associated autumn with the celebration of the

gathering of crops and fruits of the land. But with the skies darkening in preparation for winter, it is a time when all living creatures and humans begin to imagine the harshness of the cold winter period ahead.

But it is quotes from the poem by John Keats called 'Ode to Autumn' describes the season perfectly with the opening words 'Season of mists and mellow fruitfulness, close bosom-friend of the maturing sun. The season of bounteous fecundity, a time of mellow fruitfulness'. In poetical terms, he describes the season with melancholy.

Before the 16th Century the word 'Harvest' was widely used, as people were working the land and reaping the crops. But the term harvest became lost in time and was eventually replaced with expression autumn.

Traditions of the world for the Autumn Equinox are remembered with Higan, a weeklong celebration of remembrance where the custom of visiting family graves was important for the cleaning tombstones, decorating them with flowers and the burning of incense sticks. Praying for ancestors with the offering of food was a long-established tradition from an era of ancient times.

Another practice involved the gathering of crops and fruits to be blessed by the local priest and used for medicines by preserving them for the year ahead.

Feasting during the equinox was a celebration. Folk would cook a fattened goose with ginger, which was thought to be symbolic for the season. This root spice also introduced gingerbread and ginger beer, creations which are still made in today's society.

A gory ritual of the corn-spirit involved young maidens who would be given the task of cutting the last corn. Savagely, when they became older in age and bearers of children, they would be slain and buried in fields with water poured upon their graves to resemble rain charms. The blood of passing strangers was drained too and mixed with ashes and seed-corn to ward off evil spirits. They were killed in the belief that they were manifestations of the corn-spirit escaping from the freshly farmed corn. These rituals are now thankfully buried in history.

Autumnal ghostly tales seem abundant at the time of the Equinox, with the frightful spectacle of armies of Roman soldiers marching across the hillside and down into the valley accompanied by a headless horseman. These ghostly images are said to manifest at every crossroads throughout Wales at midnight on the eve of the equinox.

Old roads seem to attract mystical thieves wearing tan coloured clothing. They tramp the streets of Wales carrying sacks of stolen food on their backs whilst carrying hobby lanterns. Could these implausible images be re-enactments of dastardly deeds from days gone by, or just uncanny images of the mind?

Eerie sounds from invisible children have also been heard at this time of year, with their loud singing echoing across the land throughout the ages. But where could these sounds from children come from and why would they want to continue singing in an age beyond their time on the earth's plane?

September

September is the ninth month of the Gregorian calendar and comes from the Roman word Septem, meaning seven, as it was the seventh month of the Julian calendar. People believed that Septem was protected by the Roman god Vulcan and kept them from the perils of fire, volcanic eruptions and earthquakes.

The Anglo-Saxons called this month gest monarth meaning barley month as it was the time of the year that they could make their favourite drink barley brew through the reaping of the crops. September was also known as haefest monarth, which was the month of the harvest.

The Gregorian calendar, named after Pope Gregory XIII, was adopted in 1582, although it was not accepted by Britain until 1753. Eerily, nothing happened between 3rd and 13th of September because these days were lost during the transition and it was calculated that the earth's rotation around the sun had fallen out of line with the traditional seasons. People paraded the streets chanting *'Give us back our 11 days'*. Unfortunately they were lost forever, never to be given back.

Another custom relating to September was the calling of the mare, which was a traditional competition between farmers and their neighbours. The gathering of the last sheaf was used to make the peculiar shape of a mare which was thrown to the neighbour. The last farmer to complete this bizarre task had to display the mare beside the barn to let people know that he was the slowest farmer of the year. He would be ridiculed for the duration of the coming months.

Corn dollies were also made as symbols to the goddess of the corn; a tradition dating back hundreds of years. The goddess was believed to live within the growing corn and would die when harvested. The last cluster was used to make a corn dolly to keep her spirit alive.

Michaelmas day is traditionally the last day of the harvest and the beginning of the winter curfew. It falls on 29th when Church bells would ring out at 9 o'clock in ancient times, one strike for each day of the past year. This task would carry forward each night until Shrove Tuesday. The oldest curfew dates back to 1380.

Michaelmas is the Patron Saint of the sea, maritime, land, ships, boatsmen, horses and horsemen and is the representative of the angel who threw Lucifer (the devil) down from heaven for his evil ways. This day was also classed as goose day as a feast of good luck. Elizabeth I was consuming goose when she received news that the Spanish Armada had been defeated and she declared a feast was a celebration for all folk throughout the land and good luck would fall upon those who ate this meat on Michaelmas Day.

A prediction of the cooking of the goose revealed that if the bones were brown after roasting the winter would be mild; but if white or blue winter months would be cold and frosty.

A Michaelmas saying was chanted on the morning of the feast day and filled people with hope for luck during the year ahead: *'**Eat goose on Michaelmas Day, shan't money lack or debts to pay'***

A superstitious belief that the devil stamps or spits upon bramble bushes on this day was popular during a bygone era and blackberries were forbidden to be picked until 30th September. This was because he is said to have fallen from heaven, landing within the bramble bush and he cursed the fruit by raging his fiery breath upon the bush, stamping and spitting upon it in temper. This curse of doom is supposedly renewed annually and bad luck will besiege anyone who defies it.

During the Victorian era trees planted on harvest day would grow well and bloom. Whereas Celtic belief stated that a ring found in Michaelmas pie would predict marriage for the recipient in the coming year.

The 4th September was Holy Rood Day where children were pardoned from school or work to gather nuts, a custom which died out throughout the journey of time.

September has many memorable occasions attached to it, including the Great Fire of London which raged for 4 days from 2nd – 6th September in 1666, on 2nd 1753 Britain adopted the Gregorian calendar, Francis Drake returned to

Plymouth on the Golden Hind on 26th in 1580 and Admiral Nelson was born on 29th 1758.

Spooky tales seem to engulf the month of September, with many tales of ghostly beings lurking in the background.

The old lanes which wind from Llanharry to Aberthin are no stranger to the alarming sight of a drifting nun. She appears at dusk throughout the middle part of the month, floating down the lane before mysteriously disappearing behind the cascading trees and hedgerow. Witnesses to this spectacle in these tree-tunnelled lanes are often left bewildered as this spooky image has no relevance in today's society. Where could this nun have come from and why does she want to linger in a place that would be unrecognisable to her from a long forgotten era?

October

October is the 10th month on the Gregorian calendar and was the eighth on the Roman calendar and comes from the Latin word octo which means eight. The Welsh know it as Hydref, whereas the Anglo-Saxons called October Wintirfyllith, because of the full moon (fylleth), as winter was supposed to begin after it: in Germany they called it Wein-mond signifying the month of Wine.

On the 31st October we celebrate Halloween, which is one of the 3 spirit days when the dead are believed to roam the earth's plain. The other two are Christmas Eve and New Year's Eve. Witching hour falls at midnight on this date when these cackling sorceresses are said to plaque our skies.

But the ancient festival of Halloween (or its original title All Hallows Eve) dates back to the 16th Century (1556) and was first recognised by the Celtic Festival of Samhain, a celebration of the end of the harvest. The burning of bonfires was thought to attract insects that would become magnets to the flames of the fire and foodstuff for bats, the traditional eerie creature widely associated with Halloween.

All Hallows Eve was a festival with a Pagan background too, honouring the dead by the ringing of bells for the souls of unrest awaiting permission to enter heaven. This place of unrest is also known as purgatory. Bread and soul cakes were baked as offerings to the spirits on this day in the belief that the borders between the living and the dead would become one and the deceased would cause chaos by casting spells of sickness and damaging crops upon communities on the earth's plain. To deter this spell of evil, people would dress up in costumes and masks so that they could not be recognised by this unearthly parade of 'zombies'. This ritual was also known as guising because the people were imitating supernatural scary mortals.

Halloween is the night before All Saints Day, (1st November) and is a time when people believed that the souls of the dead would wander the earth to gain vengeance on their enemies before taking their place of rest beyond our earthly realm. The burning of candles was also thought to help these spirits to retire to their place of rest.

The Scottish poet John Mayne describes the traditions of Halloween with his poetical wording 'What fearful pranks ensue! and Bogies (ghosts)' in 1780 to reflect the fearful antics of the occasion.

Some Historians claim that the origins of Halloween come from the Roman feast of Pomona, the Goddess of fruits and seeds. This festival related to the harvest, which allegedly enticed fairies to fly through the air to signify peace.

Another symbol associated with Halloween comprised of Jack-O-Lanterns, which were carved out turnips or Swedes with burning candles inside. These were devotedly used in the belief that a blazing candle would ward off all evil. This folklore derives from a farmer of ancient times

144

who deviously trapped the devil by tricking him into climbing a tree. By placing wooden crosses around its base, the evil one would be unable to return to the ground and therefore could not implore his evil upon the living.

Other interpretations of Halloween include the depictions of death, evil, occult, mythical monsters and witches, who are said to patrol the earth on travelling contraptions resembling broomsticks on this abhorrent night.

Apple bobbing customs involved apples and candles pierced onto sticks hanging from ceilings by string. Participants of this game had their hands tied behind their backs and attempting to take a bite from the apple avoiding becoming burnt by the flame from the candle. Another variation of this entailed treacle coated scones hanging by string from the boughs of trees.

During the early 1900s, the erroneous belief of writing fortunes using milk onto white paper was popular. The dried paper was then folded and placed into a walnut or hazelnut shell and cooked on an open fire. The browned writing as it cooked over the flames would then predict the maiden's future husband.

Nos Galan Gaeaf (winter's eve in Welsh) was considered to depict the first day of winter. Traditionally Welsh families would place heavenly food on windowsills as offerings to their ancestors, whilst praying for their protection from the evils of Halloween.

Ghostly tales also seem to emulate on All Hallows Eve. The manifestations of drowned sailors ride the waves of the seas around Glamorgan as if on horseback. They are usually in visitation until the phantom bells ring out loudly from beneath the waters at midnight on this terrifying night.

Graveyards are also the target of ghostly beings, where

piercing cries emerge from the depths of the earth below in the trickery of luring the living to walk around the Church twelve times at midnight. The names of villagers who are destined to die within the year ahead are eerily chanted from beyond the grave at the last chime forecasting midnight.

Illusory fires burn upon the hillside around the villages of Wales, with spectral folk dancing around them whilst singing eerie songs in an unrecognisable language. But what could these performances be for and why would they want to bellow out chants in a dialect beyond our understanding?

November

Autumnal November is the eleventh month on the Gregorian calendar. It derives its name from the Latin word novem which means nine, as it was the ninth month on the Roman datebook.

The Welsh people know November as Tachwedd and the Anglo-Saxons 'Wind Monarth' as it was the time of year when the cold wind began to blow. They also named it 'blod monarth' as they slaughtered cattle for winter food and they would be smeared with the animals' blood. The birthstone for November is Topaz and its flower the chrysanthemum.

Poet T. S. Elliot (1888 – 1965) called it Sombre November with the quote:

"Since golden October declined into sombre November, the apples were gathered and stored and the land became brown sharp points of death in a waste of water and mud."

The first day of the month is known as All Saints Day. But in more ancient times All Hallows Day, as it followed Halloween.

Celtic tribes labelled it La Samhna, or November Day, as it was their New Year. Customs were carried out including the making of bara brith (fruit cake), cawl cennin (leek stew) and laverbread.

November 2nd was Hallowtide and was dedicated to praying for the dead. Hallow is an old word for Saint or Holy person and this day was a celebration with festivals remembering their dearly departed by visiting graves, cooking soul cakes (a modern hot cross bun minus currants) and visiting neighbours' houses singing songs accompanied by hobby horses in the belief that spirits paid visits to their old homes. Candles would also be lit and the departed's favourite meals cooked to guide them to their destinations.

The evening of 4th November was traditionally called Mischief Night during ancient times. Naughty actions were performed such as putting everyday items like pots and pans in the wrong room to confuse other members of the household.

Traditionally on November 5th bonfires would be lit in celebration of the capture of Guy Fawkes who was arrested beneath the House of Parliament as his plot to blow up King James I was uncovered in 1605. Today, we traditionally celebrate the occasion by the lighting of bonfires and firework displays.

The 11th November was Martinmas Day before World War I. Beef was customarily eaten on this date together with cake and ale for the workers. In 1918, the name was changed to Armistice Day to honour the fallen from the perils of battle.

The 22nd November was known as St. Cecilia's Day. She was believed to have been a Roman maiden who was martyred in 2nd or 3rd Centuries. She was given the status of the Patron Saint of Music as she played the organ. Her story is portrayed in 'Second Nun's Tale' in Chaucer's Canterbury Tales.

The 23rd November was Old Clem's Day which was an honourable time to celebrate St. Clement, the patron saint of blacksmiths.

The last Sunday of November was known as Stir-up Day where the Christmas pudding was made. All members of the household made a wish as it was almost the beginning of advent and arrangements for the festival of Christmas were pondered. As duck was cooked with an old saying was recited: *'Frost in November to hold a duck, the rest of the winter is slush and muck.'*

Other historic occasions which happened throughout November include the birth of astronomer Edmond Halley (8th 1656) who discovered the comet which was named after him, Dylan Thomas the flamboyant Welsh bard died at the age of 39 on 9th 1953, highwayman Jack Sheppard was hanged in London on 16th 1724 and archaeologist Howard Carter discovered the tomb of Tutankhamun on 26th 1922.

With the return of darkness following the summer months, ghostly tales are still rife around November and Moor lane in Porthcawl is no exception. This creepy lane is known for its eerie stories and has its own tales of ghosts who enjoy making their presence known around this time. The mysterious sound of church bells has been heard ringing out into the darkness from an invisible place of worship, sending shivers down the spines of its witnesses. One legend maintains that the bells from a forgotten church are rung out by legendary religious inhabitants from a bygone era. But who could these people be and why would they want to perform this deed in a place that has no relevance to such traditions today?

Phantom armies are also reported to parade the roads of Wales as if in search of something or even someone, yet no sound is ever heard.

Eerie sounds from invisible children have also been heeded at this time of year, with their loud singing echoing across the land throughout the ages. But where could these children be from and why would they want to continue singing in an age beyond their time on the earth's plain?

December

The winter month of December is the 12th month on the Gregorian calendar, although it was the 10th on the Roman datebook. December is the first month of meteorological winter in our Northern Hemisphere. It obtained its name from the Latin word 'decem' which means ten.

The Anglo-Saxons called December 'Winter Monarth' or 'Yule Monarth' as its traditions urged them to burn Yule logs. Christians at the time called it 'Heligh Monarth' which means Holy Month.

December's birthstone is blue turquoise or zircon and the recently added tanzanite. Its birth flower is the holly, narcissus or poinsettia. Its Zodiac signs are Sagittarius (until December 21) and Capricorn (December 22 until 21 January).

The first Sunday of December is the beginning of Advent which means coming. This suggests that it is the time for the preparation for the feast of Christmas which was the coming of the Lord over 2000 years ago.

The 6th was the feast day of the Bishop St. Nicholas, who was born in Turkey in 270AD. He is the Patron Saint of children. It was originally celebrated on this date in Europe to acknowledge his death on this date and he is said to have brought sweets and presents for well behaved children. The tradition quickly spread throughout the world and in America they changed his name to Santa Claus, whereas Britain adopted the term Father Christmas. The date was then altered to be celebrated towards the end of the month which closes the Advent season and initiates the twelve days of Christmastide, which ends after twelfth night on 6th January.

When the Romans introduced January and February to the calendar, they named December 26th as the Day of Goodwill. We celebrate it today as Boxing Day.

In ancient Roman times during 18th and 19th Centuries, Saturnalia (17th) was the beginning of the Roman-Pagan festival honouring their god of agriculture. This event was fêted for one day, but rapidly grew into a seven day feast of merrymaking. Slaves were treated with respect for the entire celebration by their masters and presents were exchanged, colourful clothing worn and gambling games played. The appointed Master of the Revels was aptly named Lord of Misrule who chaired the celebrations right up until 25th. Human sacrifice was also relevant to the feast, a macabre tradition now buried in history.

Pagans had always worshipped the trees of the forest and brought them into their homes to decorate with flamboyant garlands. This was the beginning of the familiar tradition of the Christmas tree.

Mistletoe and its origins come from Norse mythology where the god Balder was killed using a mistletoe arrow while fighting a rival god over a lady named Nanna.

Druids had a ritual of using mistletoe to poison their human sacrificial victim, whereas "kissing under the mistletoe" was invented as a Christian custom of love and respect for others.

The 21st December, or Winter Solstice, is the shortest day and longest night of the year. It is a Pagan festival which was also called Yule and literally means start of the winter season when the sun appears at its lowest above the horizon. Solstice (sistere) means stand still in Latin while sol means sun and the Winter Solstice, although in contrast to the Summer Solstice, has been celebrated throughout the ages. People from ancient times recognised the peculiarity of the sun and moon standing still in the sky on this date.

On 23rd a Humanist holiday is celebrated. One of the more modern creations, it celebrates the winter solstice and has been observed in this way since 2001.

The most memorable occasion in December is, of course, the festivity of Christmas. The term Christmas appeared in Old English as early as 1038 A.D. as *Cristes Maesse* and later as *Cristes-messe* in A.D. 1131. It means "the Mass of Christ." This name was established by the Christian church to disconnect the holiday and its customs from pagan origins. "We hold this day holy, not like the pagans because of the birth of the sun, but because of "Him who made it" an old saying at that time.

Christmas celebrates the birth of Our Lord and was set to the 25th December in 4th Century by the Romans. They declared this date as the birth of Christ in order to banish what they called the *'evils of the festival of Saturnalia'*. Popular modern customs include gift giving, Christmas music and carols, the exchange of Christmas cards, Christmas trees decorated in vibrant colours, fairy lights, mistletoe, wreaths, garlands and the performance of the infamous Nativity Play. It is a holiday period with a feast central to the Christian liturgical year, with merrymaking at its core. These are modern incarnations of the most depraved pagan rituals ever practiced on earth. But we still cherish them to break up the monotony of the winter season.

Winter Solstice

The winter solstice (Alban Arthan in Welsh meaning light of winter) occurs on 21st December and is the shortest day and longest night of the year when the sun appears at its lowest above the horizon. Solstice (151ateri) means stand still in

Latin while sol means sun.

Expressed as 'Midwinter's Day' during Neolithic times, it was a celebration where its people would observe the rays of the sun en-route towards sundown. The Midwinter festival was proclaimed as the last celebration of the fruitful year, because the winter months ahead were known to cause famine and misery through lack of food available from the land. Cattle and livestock were slaughtered for the feast so that they would not have to be fed during the starvation months. Wine and beer would have fermented perfectly by this time and drunk for the occasion.

The festivities began on the 20th December, the eve of the solstice, which was calculated as the beginning of the pre-Romanised winter's day. It was known as the festival of Bacchus which was toasted for the days leading up to 25th December. The consumption of wine surrounded this rather lengthy occasion because light and the rebirth of the sun was important to the people of that era.

Stone structures were built to align with the sun at certain times of the day, such as at dawn and high noon and rituals of sacrifice were performed as well as an hour of silence to honour the solstice in the hope of liberating peace. It would seem that festivals of this nature were plentiful during ancient times and possibly a further excuse for mass gatherings and merriment.

Druid customs celebrated the festival of Alban Arthuan on 21st December as a time of death and rebirth. They believed that souls of the dead would be given a new lease of life on this date because the sun of the New Year would be reborn the following morning. They also regarded mistletoe as sacred and kissing beneath it was a pledge of friendship. The occasion was followed by Yuletide, an earlier term for the Christmas celebration.

Author Richard Heinberg (a modern writer) describes the winter solstice as 'times of danger and opportunity;

times for special alertness and aliveness. Wisdom consists of knowing one's place in any given cycle and what kinds of action are appropriate for that phase', quotes which portray the time of year to perfection.

Hauntings around the time of the Winter Solstice are not the typical zombified apparitions often associated with festivals, but tales of folklore and legends yearning to be remembered.

The Celtic custom of the Sluagh-Sidhe (people of the Sidhe) included haunted mounds or barrows where the souls of the dead were said to rebound from one world into another and faeryfolk (fairies) entered magical castles. Celtic tribes would lay the bones of the dead to rest upon the mounds to release their souls into another world beyond our realm.

Spirits of the Yule during Celtic times included the Mysterious Stranger which was the manifestation of the ghostly image of baby Jesus. Witnessing this Mysterious Stranger was thought to be a symbol of good luck for spreading kindness and goodwill to all men. But it was during the later part of the Celtic era that St. Thomas, the Apostle to Jesus Christ, was honoured too.

Eerily, the spirit of the Yule is said to become evident in the depths of the flames of fire and the Celts would carry out chants of wisdom with the words *'life begins in a spark; a fire is the light of the soul'*. This is when the Yule tree (pine) representing the powers of life was adopted to invite pleasant Yuletide spirits from the outer world to join them on earth. The Yule tree originally came from Germany and was traditionally decorated with colourful objects just before midnight on 13th December. At the stroke of midnight singing and dancing in a circle rotating clockwise became popular as a practice used for seeing out the old sun and welcoming in the new. This would evoke the spirits of the dead to dance around the stones, or so the fable states.

Phantom bells are reported to ring out across the land at midnight on the dawn of the rebirth of the sun, yet no Church is known to be engaged in this activity. Could the spirits of yesteryear be challenging the living to re-establish their ancient customs? And do these traditions ring true?

The Story of Ghosts

I have been writing about ghosts and the paranormal for many years and one question which always arises caused me to think of answers. What are ghosts and why do they visit to us on earth?

The word ghost probably comes from the Old English word gost, which means breath or spirit, and was described as misty white vapourised figures.

Ghosts as we perceive them appear to us in many forms. But apparitions, which have been described as the energy of a deceased person or animal, are unwilling or unable to leave the earth's atmosphere and move to the higher realms beyond our understanding. This could be because they do not recognise that they are actually dead, have died in traumatic or emotional circumstances, or were even perpetrators of crime where their evil

spirit is said to be unwelcome in the world outside our human existence.

I would say that apparitions are probably the most common of experiences with phantoms as I have encountered such specters through years of ghost hunting with the Porthcawl Paranormal Team. We have investigated many public places throughout Porthcawl and beyond over the years and have connected with an array of unearthly beings, although we have never emanated fear towards them.

My first ever experience happened on a casual evening in a public house in New Road, Porthcawl where I saw a young girl in Victorian dress emerge through a wall and disappear through another behind me in the ladies toilets.

The team discovered a few years later that she had tragically drown in an ancient well whilst collecting water.

Ghosts do not always express themselves in what appears to be physical form but have also been known to make their presence known by releasing smells such as perfurme, odour, food and drink into the atmosphere. An instance for the Paranormal Team was inside a public house in Newton where an unusual smell of sweet tobacco became prominent. This was intriguing as it was a year after the smoking ban had become law, so no earthly person could have executed this aroma.

Ghosts are not always seen in full view and can often present themselves as disembodied, which means that only part of their anatomy is displayed. This could be because their body was not complete when they died and that they are in search of their remaining appendage. But in some cases, ghosts appear with the intent of harming the living whichever way they choose to 156aterialize.

However, demonic spiritual entities have also been encountered where the feeling of malevolence in a darker form is propelled. Their intent is to spread fear and harm to the innocent, mainly in particular locations where they have become trapped. This type of ghost is thought to enter our atmosphere through a vortex which is an invisible whirlpool of light to the naked eye. But could these be tricks of the mind of an overactive imagination, or simply an indication that afterlife really does exist?

Ghosts are not committed to time and can appear at any stage during the day or night. In fact, over ⅔ of sightings occur during the afternoon, banishing the myth that they materialize during the hours of darkness or even only on the night of Halloween, a night in the calendar year dedicated to ghosts, ghouls and demons which are said to haunt our earthly realm.

It may be possible that this type of spirit is looking for

someone or something which was special to them during their time on the earth's plain, or that they have not found peace within their outer spiritual body. In this case communication with them is usually experimented with as ghostly forms only appear for a short period of time before vanishing into thin air. The Porthcawl Paranormal Team have often integrated with ghosts through the power of asking questions, therefore prompting them to communicate by performing knocks or bangs of one for yes and two for no.

Ghosts also have the power to move objects, a sometimes exciting and intriguing action to witness. This is known as poltergeist activity.

Whatever our belief is in ghosts and their actual existence, would you really want to disregard their intrusion on our earth's plain because who knows what may happen if you do?

Pirates and Smugglers of the Glamorgan Coast

Pirates and smugglers were rife throughout the whole of the Glamorgan coast during the 18th Century, as with other locations around the world. Some infamous and ruthless individuals were William Arthur and Thomas Knight who set up their control centre on Barry Island. They plagued the shores and Thomas Knight, the notorious smuggler, built barricades around the island to isolate his base so that his fleet of ships (which were heavily armed) circulated fear amongst locals.

He would charge along the Bristol Channel to destinations such as the Channel Islands where alcohol and tobacco were looted as they were considered to be luxury items at the time. He also acquired soap from Ireland in a dastardly way.

Thomas Knight is documented at his stronghold in Barry in 1783 as travelling to other destinations beyond our shores on his ship called the John O'Combe, equip with a vast quantity of armoury and 60-70 crew. He managed to outwit the Customs Authorities and gain respect from local people probably because he could sell on his wares amongst them. Because of this he adopted the nickname 'The King of Smuggling'.

Knight's reign was short-lived however as in 1785, the Authorities managed to outwit him for his illegal trade and he fled to Lundy Island. He is said to have died there a very wealthy man.

Islands are undoubtedly visible from the mainland in

clear weather and this notorious trade could be seen in full view during the hours of daylight. And although the Customs Authorities were aware of the wrongdoings around the shorelines, they were powerless to halt it as they did not have a boat to journey across the water at the beginning of this scandalous trade.

Flat Holm Island in the middle of the Bristol Channel, was an ideal location for the illicit trade of smuggling. This unlawful industry became rife during the 18th Century and it is thought that an old mine shaft on the northern side of the island was an ideal base for smugglers to hoard their loot from both England and Wales.

A small cave on the eastern side had natural tunnels giving easy access to the sea. This cave in the easterly cliff became a storage point for contraband, kegs of brandy and tea. In fact, a local writer from 1902 commented in his writings that

'The men are still living who claimed to have seen (the cave) filled with that had never paid the Queen's dues'.

It is doubtful that the author of this observation visited the island as the cave has the characteristics of being too small for human activity and this amount of loot would barely fit into such a confined chamber. However, smuggling probably did exist on the island as the old mine shaft was littered with tunnels and the exit was disguised as solid rock.

There were many more haunts for this illegal trade along the coast which include Sully, Swanbridge, Cadoxton-juxta , Barry, Penarth Head, Aberthaw, Llantwit Major, Nash Point, Dunraven, Southerndown and Porthcawl, to name but a few.

Other infamous Welsh pirates/smugglers operating along the Glamorgan coast that spread fear throughout communities were Modryb Sina (Aunt Sina) Howel Davies, Black Bart Roberts, Bartholomew, Colin Dolphyn and Jack Callis.

But during the latter part of 18th Century, the illustrious trade had petered out and many believe the Customs Authorities had tightened their grip on a coast littered with such rogues.

Our coastline has seen its fair share of illegal scoundrels and because of their deeds it would seem inevitable that tales of their ghosts plague our shores.

Invisible but chilling screams have been heard, bellowing out across the seas pitifully shouting for help, which could only have fallen upon deaf years from a bygone era, when looters gleefully watched the harrowing ordeal of innocent sailors drowning in the cruel sea. Could these haunting sounds be from restless seaman walking the coastline in search of help?

At Kymin House in Penarth, the ghostly figure of an 18th Century pirate is reported to reside. He seems to enjoy remaining on the earth's plain, scaring people with his rebellious dress and brutal-looking face. But who could this mutinous man be and why does haunting in this way give him satisfaction?

On the distant seas towards Sker rocks in Porthcawl, a ghostly ship has been seen mirroring white mist around it, particularly on stormy nights, when mysterious Church bells will distinctly ring out. Could these scary happenings be a reenactment of a ship lost to the treacherous seas when the bells would ring out warning its people of disaster?

At Barry Island the ghost of a local pirate is said to haunt the entire area, seemingly patrolling the coast as if trying to protect inhabitants from foreign invaders. Could this be the ghost of a local hero called Benedict y Diffoddwrr whose ship was attacked by Spanish pirates, or another outlaw whose fate remains unknown?

Rhonnda Cynon Taf

Llanharan

The community of Llanharan lies in the Border Vale between Llanharry and Brynna and is in fact in the county of Rhondda Cynon Taf. It has changed considerably over the years, but still holds some memorable landmarks which display some of its original agricultural buildings. Many features are now a distant memory such as the dairy, cinema, police station, undertakers, 2 billiard halls, a library, bakery, bank, garage and coal merchant, some of which I remember as a child, particularly the appealing shops and the bakery, which sold mouthwatering bread and cakes run by the Richardson family. The shops all ceased trade one by one and Llanharan was labelled a *'ghost town'* during 1980s.

The Grade II listed Llanharan House sits proudly on the hill overlooking Llanharan village. Built in 1750 by Rees Powell it remained within his family until 1795 when Richard Hoare Jenkins purchased the property and launched the Llanharan fox hunt by 1805. After his death in 1856, the estate was taken over by Colonel John Blandy-Jenkins and remained in his family until 1953.

The Welsh spaniel dogs are thought to have been originally bred here, another legend concerning Llanharan's history. Nicknamed the Llanharan spaniel, its image was adopted as the logo for Llanharan Rugby Club which formed in 1891. Rugby union was originally played on the pitch called 'The Diaryfield but has now been moved to the plot where the British Legion Club once stood.

Llanharan square is a rewarding sight with some charming historical buildings, including the ancient public house which was built around 1700 and served as a chapel during the era when going to Church was deemed a necessity.

During 1880s the village became associated with coal mining at the Powell Duffryn Company (PDs) which was part of the Meiros colliery, but now just a distant memory. A small railway station was opened in 1850 to accommodate steam trains, allowing travel to more distant shores for residents. My mother, Gaynor Stallard, remembered the excitement felt by children from local Sunday schools who enjoyed travelling on the train to Porthcawl for their annual day trip. Sadly, Dr. Richard Beeching closed many railways throughout the United Kingdom in 1964 and Llanharan station became deserted until December 2007 when it was reopened for the public to enjoy travelling by rail once more.

Legendary folk tales are still rife throughout the village, although some have now been buried in history. The Brenin Llwyd, or Grey Monarch of the mists, was a typical tale from the depths of time. He is said to live amongst the hills and prey on innocent ramblers by drawing them into his curse of bewilderment.

Llanharan house stands eerily in the darkness and the legend of 3 witches prowling the hills around it has been the subject of scandal since ancient times. It is not known who they were or if they actually existed, but could they still be lurking on the hilltop hoping to cast their spell on new victims from a modern world beyond their grasp?

The spectral figure of a dark-haired man has been identified standing on the corner in the square, evidently pointing towards the church on the hill. Who could this gentleman be and why would he want to linger around a village that he would no longer recognise?

The spine-chilling echo of a stagecoach travelling at pace has been heard, tearing down old Llanharry lane at dusk, forcing bystanders to violently jump from its path, only to discover that nothing of this nature is travelling through. Could this frightful noise be a hurried re-enactment from a bygone era when horse and carriage was the only means of transport? As a child I was once an innocent victim to this strange occurrence.

Llantrisant Castle

Established in 1246 by Richard de Clare, Earl of Gloucester and Lord of Glamorgan, (and like Llanharan lies within the boundaries of Rhondda Cynon Taf) Llantrisant castle was built on the site of a 6th Century wooden fortification and motte erected by Gwrgan ap Ithel on the hilltop. This strengthened stone structure was used as an administration centre for the Lords of Glamorgan ruling the districts of Meisgun and Glyn Rhondda.

The castle consisted of North and South towers surrounding the oval court with the North tower called The Raven which had an elaborate doorway. It was probably circular with a horseshoe shaped bailey and a high curtain wall from a drum tower.

The likely site of the bailey is thought to have been to the North end of the castle, but no evidence of its earthwork has survived.

In 1262, Richard's son Gilbert nicknamed 'The Red' had become the occupier of the castle which almost immediately came under attack from followers of Llywelyn ap Gruffydd and was later received damaged from 4 other battles with the Welsh. This military stronghold was was said to be the second most important castle to Cardiff and was involved in the uprising of Norman Overlords led by Madog ap Llwelyn in 1294.

The castle was attacked once again in 1315 by Llywelyn Bren and his revolutionary soldiers. By 1404 Owain Glyndwr attacked and almost demolished Llantrisant castle. But it was John Leland who wrote about its ruinous state in

1536, declaring *'a fair castle with 2 wardes with inner dike and yren made in the area'.*

Edward II was imprisoned at Llantrisant castle for a short period of time under the guardianship of Constable Robert de Aston before his murder elsewhere.

An intriguing plaque dons the landscape commemorating the 650th anniversary of the granting of a Charter and the presence of Long bowmen from the Battle of Crecy in 1346. This was the Royal Charter awarded to Llantrisant allowing the community the freedom to trade without paying tolls for crossing its boundaries. The Long bowmen mentioned were known as the Black Army after their survival from the French Wars of 14th Century. They served under the banner of the Black Prince.

'Beating the Bounds' is a tradition which dates back to 1346, where children were bounced onto boundary stones by their elders. This custom would be performed every 7 years and is still practiced; the last being in 2010. The intention is to remind people of the importance of borough boundaries.

The nearby Tarren Deusant is a Pagan site and displayed 2 carvings of faces to commemorate two Saints in 1696. When completing his writings in 1979, a gentleman named Sharp claimed that 4 more had appeared in mysterious circumstances, placing their materialization into uncertainty. Could their appearance be from the phantom dragons that are deemed to roam the area, shyly leaving reminders of their continued residence on the earth's plain?

This region is also said to attract ghoulish giants, witches and fairies. But would this site be at risk of phantom overcrowding across the hills with **their** spiritual presence?

Legend maintains that William Price, an eccentric 19th Century doctor, performed Druid ceremonies on the hillside. He outlived his son and repulsed Christian burial, choosing to burn his son's body in a field, causing public outcry and disbelief. Could his strange actions be the birth of the cremation of the deceased?

At the dead of night, the ghostly form of an attractive lady is reported to haunt a particular cottage upon the hillside by eerily sitting amongst the branches of an imaginary tree. It is believed that this lingering spirit is Betty Morgan from Tal y Garn Fawr, which is situated 4 miles north of Cowbridge. But questions remain as to why she still resides in an area that she could no longer call home.

The hills around where the castle once stood contain the disfigured image of a ghostly young girl wearing a white robe, seemingly scattering roses around the area. Legend states that a witness to this lifelike figure recovered the flowers and took them home to place them in water. The following morning the roses had vanished and had been replaced with golden coins.

The frightful figure of a headless lady accompanied by a medieval soldier has been seen around the ruined tower of the castle, only to disappear in a hazy mist. Who could these ghostly folk be and why would they want to return to a place beyond their own realm?

The Floods of the Bristol Channel

On 30th January 1607 large floods occurred from the Bristol Channel and Severn Estuary covering Newport, Cardiff, Chepstow, Monmouthshire and as far afield as Carmarthenshire. Somerset and Devon were also affected by this unusual but life threatening catastrophe.

This devastating and unexpected phenomenon was cataclysmic and claimed the lives of around 2-3,000 people and countless livestock from the numerous farmland caught up in this destructive incident, which has more recently been described as a possible tsunami.

Nobody knows the real reason for such an incident, which resulted in rapid water rushing inland with sparks emulating on top of the everlasting waves. But it was described in accounts and documentation from the time as **'The Killer Wave of 1607'** caused by a vertical displacement of the seabed, or an earth tremor triggering landslides.

With such a life changing and death defying occurrence on what was thought to be a normal morning, it is very chilling to have writings of peoples' speedy reactions to such disastrous events.

In Newport, a wealthy lady named Mistress Van was drowned in her home as she did not have any time to escape the torrent of dashing water. This gives us an indication of the sprinting tide at that time. Her eerie ghost is said to haunt the area where her home once stood.

Another tale of heartache involves a 4 year old maide child whose naked mother found time to hoist her onto a beam within the home to save her from drowning before she perished in the rapid rising water. A chicken is said to have flown up to the child to save her from the rush of water which is an eerie thought from a supposedly unintelligent animal.

A similar type of account states that a baby in a cradle was saved by the pet cat which leapt from one side of the cradle to the other to help it float on the rising current of water. A quote from the scriptures at the time states the words *'as if she had been appointed steersman to preserve the small barke from the waves furie'.*

An additional story of survival involved a man and woman (possibly husband and wife) who both clambered up a tree espying death before their eyes. The surge of water seemed to miraculously rest upon the tree and carry them to safety onto drier land. With such an exceptional tale of survival, who are we to dispute this haunting account of escaping death?

Eventually, the Rt. Honourable Lord Herbert Earl of Pembroke, sent an throng of boats to rescue as many survivors as possible. He tried to relieve their distress by handing out parcels of meat and other provisions in the wake of this unusual and devastating disaster. It is said that eerie mists occurred after he had completed his generous mission.

A number of Flood Plaques were erected and still remain, to commemorate the devastation and loss of life to the barbaric floods of 1607. They show how high the water actually rose, reaching speeds of 30mph, heights of 25 feet above sea level and reaching up to 4 miles inland. Eyewitnesses described the surge of water as *'being faster than a greyhound can run'.* One such brass plaque was situated near to the altar of St. Mary's Church in Goldcliff near Newport. The Church was built in the 1080s and founded by Robert Fitzhamon. After the floods subsided the Church was described as being in ruins. The tower, foundations and roof collapsed and washed away in the forceful tidal wave. The roofless Church was abandoned in 1701 with the Prince of Wales theatre erected in its place. Today it is a public house. The plaque from the Church reads:

'1606 ON TE XX DAY INVARY EVEN AS IT CAME TO
PAS IT PLEASED GOD TE FLVD DID FLOW TO TE
EDGE OF THIS SAME BRAS * AND IN THIS PARISH
THERE WAS LOST 5000 AND OD POUNDS BESIDES
XX 11 PEOPLE WAS IN THIS PARISH DROWN

GOLDCLIF JOHN*OF PILDREW AND

WILLIAM TAP CHVRCH WAS DEAS

1609

The dates are different on the plaque as the Julian calendar was in existence at that time and when the New Gregorian calendar came into existence, as it is today, 13 extra days were added to the year. However, it took 300 years to set it in place as it only started in 1582. The New Year did not begin until 25th March under the Julian calendar and was called Lady Day. The calendar change confused the people of that time and they were furious with the extra days added and as many were illiterate back then, it gives an indication of how inaccurate their calculations had become during that time.

References

1. Buildings of Special Architectural Interest by CADW.
2. Newton Nottage and Porthcawl by Leonard S Higgins. MA
3. Cardiff and District Directory 1899.
4. Worrall's Directory 1875.
5. Kelly's Directory of South Wales
6. Central Glamorgan Gazette on microfilm at the library, Bridgend
7. Porthcawl at War 1939 -1945 by Mike Mansley.
8. Legends of Porthcawl and the Glamorgan Coast by Alun Morgan.
9. Porthcawl Historic Museum.
10. Burrows Pointer Guide Map of Porthcawl.
11. 12 Folk Tales of Pyle and Kenfig by Barrie Griffiths
12. Buildings of Special Architectural Interest by CADW.
13. Porthcawl, Newton and Nottage by Alun Morgan.
14. Around Porthcawl, Newton and Nottage by Keith Morgan.
15. Hunts and Company Directory and Topography 1849.
16. Cardiff and District Directory 1899
17. Worralls Directory 1875.

Lightning Source UK Ltd.
Milton Keynes UK
UKHW020701260521
384397UK00007B/227